SCHOOLS OF F

SCHOOLS OF HOPE

*a new agenda for
school improvement*

Terry Wrigley

Trentham Books
Stoke on Trent, UK and Sterling USA

Trentham Books Limited

Westview House	22883 Quicksilver Drive
734 London Road	Sterling
Oakhill	VA 20166-2012
Stoke on Trent	USA
Staffordshire	
England ST4 5NP	

First published 2003

British Library Cataloguing-in-Publication Data
A catalogue record for this book is available from the British Library

ISBN 1 85856 302 X

Designed and typeset by Trentham Print Design Ltd., Chester and printed in Great Britain by Cromwell Press Ltd., Wiltshire.

Have our schools been driven towards efficiency rather than genuine improvement? What really matters: new targets to meet? higher maths grades perhaps? or caring and creative learners, a future, a sense of justice, the welfare of the planet and its people?

(Editorial, *Improving Schools*, Autumn 2001)

The future of teaching is in the hands of those who turn hope into an active virtue.

(Andy Hargreaves and Michael Fullan 1998)

Contents

Introduction

Teaching is a profession of hope. We are driven by desires – for our students to discover a taste for learning, a feel for justice and care for each other. We aspire to turn children into thoughtful, creative and concerned citizens. Inspirational teachers are motivated by their dreams of a better world.

The desire to improve education arises naturally from our engagement with the future. We recognise material limitations, but cannot allow ourselves to be half-hearted. Good teachers are never satisfied with dull environments, hostile relationships, and methods that bore or confuse.

School improvement is integral to a teacher's professionalism. It is an expression of our hope for better schools and better lives. It rejects the cynicism which blames children for their lack of success; it refuses a sociological determinism which says simply that the poor are *bound* to fail. As a new field of study and set of practices, it has focused valuable attention on the positive factors which enhance learning, in schools as institutions and cultures.

School improvement has attracted a weighty literature and a throng of enthusiasts, but also much anxiety. We need to ask why, for many teachers, School Improvement (with capital letters now, almost hyphenated) seems like an alien force imposed from outside and above. It is too easy to write off teachers' genuine concerns as signs of idleness or indifference to the plight of young learners, especially those from disadvantaged backgrounds. Conversely some critics of the School Improvement project seem to suggest that improvements are just a trick with mirrors. Both responses serve to polarise and freeze discussion.

I wish to make clear from the start my hope for better schools. I have seen inspiring evidence of schools which are making a real difference to children's futures and the life of the whole community. I have experienced inner-city schools which are vibrant with hope in the midst of poverty. This book arises not from any doubts about the possibility of improvement, and certainly not about its necessity, but from serious misgivings about the current agenda for change. *Schools of Hope* invites a new direction in theory and practice.

I

School Improvement has developed a sophisticated understanding of leadership and change management, but for all its talk of vision and values, it has given little thought to the purpose of education and has largely neglected social justice. Consequently, it has not been able to challenge some of the superficial and misdirected advice from government agencies and a regime of accountability which is profoundly inequitable in its discourse and its effects. We not only have to engage in a scrutiny of School Improvement as academic literature but also to confront it as a nexus of mutually reinforcing policies, structures and actions. Among more positive consequences:

• it creates illusions of being able to overcome the problems of an increasingly polarised society through education alone

• it actively penalises those who are teaching and learning in marginalised communities

• it trivialises learning, making it increasingly difficult to challenge injustice and understand the powerful global forces which structure our lives

• it limits the scope of teachers to develop meaningful learning for working-class and ethnic minority pupils, or indeed any pupils who have difficulty in learning

• it deprofessionalises teachers, undermining the collegiality and reflection needed for real change, while giving headteachers illusory power within a wider game in which they are simply dancing to someone else's tune.

In England especially – a testbed since the early nineties – School Improvement is in deep crisis; it has become associated with a high-stress efficiency drive marked by increasing attainment gaps, superficial learning and disaffection among teachers and pupils alike. While academic experts speak increasingly of distributed leadership and transforming school cultures, government agencies reinforce the top-down pressures of accountability and surveillance. Under pressure from the dominant agenda for improvement, issues such as active citizenship and social inclusion are marginalised.

It is over ten years now since Jean Rudduck said we should talk less about the *management* of change and more about the *meaning* of change (Rudduck 1991). This neatly encapsulates much of the present difficulty. Improvement should be an ethical project, not just a technical one. This is clearly signalled by the frequent use of words such as *mission*, *vision* and *values* in the literature, yet somehow a discourse has been constructed which hollows out these words.

Effective schooling and the school improvement movement is blind to a searching interrogation of outcome. Test scores become ends . . . Explicit discussions of values and the types of society to which schools articulate/ adhere are ignored. (Slee and Weiner 1998: 111)

Widening the horizons

For school leaders working in Britain, it is all too easy to assume that one particular model of improvement is universal. England suffers particularly from a dominant version of School Improvement which has been grafted on to the statistically-based School Effectiveness paradigm. This model is well matched to an education system based on strong centralised control over state-funded schools which enjoy a notional autonomy within a competitive market – the product of Thatcher and Baker's Education Reform Act of 1988. The Anglo-American model of School Improvement has had some influence elsewhere, including parts of Australia, Hong Kong, Taiwan and to some extent the Netherlands, though even in Scotland and parts of Canada and the USA it is heavily contested. In England, where this model receives powerful government support, the situation is pregnant with contradiction – oppressive surveillance alongside breathtaking innovation, demoralisation undermining dedication, an official discourse which muddles 'pressure and support', education ministers who talk inclusion while stigmatising inner-city schools.

One of the greatest ironies is that such great concern is expressed about low achieving schools, but so little real attention given to understanding the dynamics of education and improvement in locations of dire poverty. I choose this word, rather than sheltering behind the euphemism of low socioeconomic status, to emphasise that nearly one in three children in Britain are being brought up in poverty. In some areas, it is far worse – half the pupils in inner London schools are now growing up below the poverty line. The situation is particularly severe in Britain and America, but occurs in other developed countries. The core texts of School Improvement have, in practice, largely marginalised this issue, and the relationship between underachievement and poverty remains inadequately researched and poorly theorised.

The all-pervasive Improvement project in England and Wales over the last decade has done nothing to narrow the attainment gap between rich and poor. Indeed, a name and shame culture has made life intolerable for teachers in troubled areas. Despite the constant pressure to raise targets, and the political rhetoric that 'poverty is no excuse', official data confirms the near impossibility, under the present regime, for schools in poorer areas even to reach the national average (Ofsted 2000). We are far from properly understanding what to do about this, though I will argue that the task is impossible within the current policy straitjacket.

In an earlier book, *The Power to Learn*, I explored the hypothesis that what really drives improvement in schools serving marginalised inner-city communities is not the mechanisms of top-down control but a culture of *empowerment*. This can be seen operating in the interlinking spheres of teaching and learning, curriculum, school ethos, relationships with parents and the wider community, and school development pro-cesses. Through ten case studies of successful schools with large numbers of bilingual pupils of mainly South Asian heritage, I was able to trace a socially critical discourse and practice which actively challenged dis-advantage and discrimination. Each of the headteachers and the many other leaders in these schools have a sense of educational vision that is rooted in a cultural, social and political understanding of their environ-ment (Wrigley 2000).

Despite the top–down control of the official discourse, thoughtful school leaders seek to develop collegiality and reflection in their schools and connect their educational vision to a social understanding. They struggle on a daily basis to make sense of the unspoken contradictions in the sea of advice that buffets them. They may survive by cherry-picking good ideas and quotations, but the appearance that school improvement experts are somehow singing in harmony is confusing. An honest debate would be healthier and more enlightening.

We would also benefit from opening our horizons. The Scandinavian emphasis on education for democracy has led to very different models of evaluation, leadership and development. In transatlantic collaboration, the editorial team of Andy Hargreaves and Michael Fullan (Canada) Ann Lieberman (USA) and David Hopkins (England) significantly chose to name their two-volume anthology *International Handbook of Educational Change* (1998). It includes a section labelled School Improvement, but this is located within wider perspectives around the (mainly) English-speaking world. Similar breadth of vision is shown in the *Handbook of School Development* (*Handbuch zur Schulentwicklung*, Altrichter, Schley and Schratz, eds, 1998). I am not suggesting that other education systems are unaffected by a globalising trend towards greater control of schools and the amoral ideology of economic rationalism, but even a scan of the chapter headings of these books indicates a greater understanding of the connection between theories of school development, pedagogy, human development and social justice than characterises most English texts.

In Germany, a strategic conference *Future of education – school of the future* (Bildungskommission NRW 1995) is having enduring influence in many schools. The language is radically different from the lists of 'key characteristics' of 'effective schools', or even the process models of much school improvement literature. The conference's final declaration begins with a vision of future schools:

School is a House of Learning

- a place where everybody is welcome, where learners and teachers are accepted in their individuality
- a place where people are allowed time to grow up, to take care of one another and be treated with respect
- a place whose rooms invite you to stay, offer you the chance to learn, and stimulate you to learn and show initiative
- a place where diversions and mistakes are allowed, but where evaluation in the form of feedback gives you a sense of direction
- a place for intensive work, and where it feels good to learn
- a place where learning is infectious.

This agenda for improvement begins with a rich sense of vision and values, rather than a one-dimensional focus on examination results.

These are not the only models. Thomas Sergiovanni (1999) argues the importance of building schools as communities, rather than bureaucratic or market models of schooling in which low-trust mechanisms for improvement result in short-term superficial change. Per Dalin (1998), one of the most experienced writers on wide-scale reform, derives an agenda for school improvement by looking at the dramatic social and technological change currently taking place. Paulo Freire's enduring influence in Latin America and elsewhere should not be underestimated either.

A grounded hope

To some readers it may seem strange to use the concept of *hope* as a leading principle for a book on school improvement. We are used to models of science – in social sciences too – which claim objectivity by denying subjectivity. Imitating a positivist discourse from the physical sciences, we strip our writing of emotion and identity to make it more 'theoretical'. Such 'objectivity' is difficult to sustain in discussions of educational change; the personal histories, narratives of lived events, emotional crises and political beliefs push up like wild flowers between the flagstones.

I recently re-read Christopher's Hill's account of the growth of science and technology in the period leading to the English Revolution of the 1640s. Francis Bacon is often portrayed as the father of a modern scientific paradigm which is ruthlessly instrumental and denies moral values. In reality his historic role was much more to relate the project of scientific advance to a progressive moral purpose. Reacting against the pessimism and timeless truths of the medieval world-view, he believed that scientific method would help liberate mankind from the consequences of 'the Fall'. He hoped for 'a restitution and reinvigorating (in great part) of man to the sovereignty and power . . . which he had in his first state of creation'. For Bacon, the pursuit of knowledge was an act of charity. Knowledge should not be sought as . . .

> a couch, whereupon to rest a searching and restless spirit; or a terrace, for a wandering and variable mind to walk up and down with a fair prospect; or a tower of state for a proud mind to raise itself upon; or a fort or commanding ground, for strife and contention; or a shop for profit and sale. [It should be] a rich storehouse, for the glory of the Creator, and the relief of man's estate. (Hill 1965: 89–94)

Present-day ecologists are no less scientific for their passionate commitment; critics of globalisation do not lose their theoretical edge when they speak to a wide public. Conversely, when natural and social scientists are silent on issues of morality and politics, they often allow their work to be abused by the very forces they are too polite to mention.

By hope, I do not mean a rosy optimism, an emotional inner glow. That would be difficult indeed at this time. I mean a grounded hope which arises out of a full recognition of material and social needs and possibilities. As educators, we need a hope which dares to confront our troubled world.

To adopt a purely technical discourse of school improvement is not just a question of style, it is a political choice. When school improvers fail to address the context and goals of education, their project becomes a mere efficiency drive. We must keep asking 'to what ends?' and 'for whose benefit?'

The question of educational aims lies at the heart of any real understanding of improvement. How can we know if schools are improving unless we decide what they should be good for? The problem has become even more acute in the aftermath of 11 September 2001. Struggling to put together an editorial for the journal *Improving Schools* in the week after a major peace demonstration in my city, I wrote as follows:

> The normal concerns of this journal seem lightweight compared with the far-reaching consequences of 11 September. The murderous demolition of the Twin Towers; the world's most powerful president launching a 'crusade' against enemies yet to be named; the world plunged into a war which some US politicians threaten may last 50 years . . .
>
> There is discussion everywhere, as the young (and not so young) surge forward to question and debate – an unexpected education. Young people everywhere (the 'apathetic generation'?) are asking difficult questions, making new connections – why sanctions are killing Iraqi children, what leads to the blind anger of terrorism, what are cluster bombs, the geo-politics of oil in Central Asia, the tentacles of globalised power, the World Trade Organisation, Third World debt, religion, hunger, civilisation, peace.
>
> This puts into a new perspective our brave attempts to improve our schools. We have devoted such energy to developing a sophisticated knowledge of change management, planning, assessment, school cultures, leadership. Now, in this new century, the question is unavoidably – *to what end, all this?* Where is the *vision?*
>
> 'Economic rationalism' (which is, of course, not entirely separate from other features of globalisation) is facing a growing international critique. Much of the high-level government interest in school improvement has led to an intensification of teaching, accountability, league tables, teachers feeling deprofessionalised and disenchanted (or leaving), a relentless drive for more though not always better – and silence on the question of *educational purpose.*
>
> What really matters: new targets to meet? higher maths grades perhaps? or caring and creative learners, a future, a sense of justice, the welfare of the planet and its people?

Improvement built on hope reaches out, unblinkered, to a fast-changing and troubled world; it has a concreteness and specificity which neutral discussions of change management cannot touch. To examine school improvement using the touchstone of *hope* is not a vaguely utopian moralism but an attempt to reconnect to core issues. Hope is a principle which unites the actions and aspirations of teachers, parents, children and headteachers. It enables us to understand 'high expectations' not as top-down numerical targets but as educational and political challenges within specific social contexts. It articulates connections between the five key areas of school development, curriculum, pedagogy, ethos and the wider community which school leaders need to align in order to bring about significant change.

This book is necessarily theoretical as well as practical; it moves between sharp critique and inspirational examples of practice. Theoretical debate helps to dispel confusion and clarify action. It may appear negative for the early chapters to develop a critique of the dominant paradigms of School Effectiveness and School Improvement and the accompanying practices of accountability and performance management, but this is needed to clear the fog. A theoretical response to current policy directions and taken-for-granted practices will hopefully strengthen resistance.

Recent research into school leadership processes and change management has brought valuable new understandings, but it can lead to confusion when divorced from an analysis of the wider environment. Educational change does not occur in a vacuum. Many school leaders try hard to make coherent sense of a plethora of advice, seeking to assimilate diverse and contradictory messages as if they were somehow additive. They struggle to reconcile inspirational quotations from Fullan with the government's latest dose of top-down directives and target setting. Understandably, many headteachers are finding it hard to disentangle the unacknowledged contradictions or to navigate the political cross-currents.

My hope is to provide some greater coherence to our understanding of improvement, to disentangle the weeds from the daisies, to relate school change to what is happening in the wider world, and to facilitate communication among a professional community with its heart set on a better future. It will draw upon fields of educational study which mainstream school improvement studies have tended to overlook.

Outline of chapters

The first section, *Critiques*, questions the assumptions behind current orthodoxy. Chapter 1 *School effectiveness: the problem of reductionism* analyses the attempt to subsume educational evaluation within the hard science of statistics. Research which seeks to use statistical correlation to identify why some schools are more 'effective' is often assumed to provide a common-sense foundation for the Improvement project. I believe it is methodologically flawed, presents an oversimplified view of the social context of schools, and avoids questions of educational and social values. The chapter includes references to alternative examples of quantitative research which are sidelined because they are politically off message.

Chapter 2 *School improvement: where do we go from here?* begins a critique of the dominant model of School Improvement which is grounded in the ideological foundations of School Effectiveness. England in particular has been its testbed for the past ten years. Government agencies claim to base their recommendations on sound academic theory, though in practice official policy bears only a superficial relationship to the best available research on change processes, extracting from it only what suits. The chapter examines the anti-democratic consequences of following this dominant model, arguing for a more conscious sense of social and educational direction, in theory and in practice.

The next section, *Dilemmas*, moves the discussion forward by examining school improvement in relation to school cultures and structures. Chapter 3 *Commitment or surveillance: the ecology of change* contrasts developmental cultures based on engaged professionalism with the low-trust accountability regimes which stifle initiative and undermine morale. It calls for a reculturing of schools through empowered and creative leadership at all levels.

Chapter 4 *Whose improvement? whose schools?* highlights the dangers when School Improvement ignores major policy shifts. England's New Labour politicians now disparage the very idea of comprehensive schools, and engage in modernisation plans which always seems to involve privatising. The privatisation of essential public services is being vigorously promoted across the world by the lead agencies of finance capital, the World Bank and International Monetary Fund, and the gulf between rich and poor is deepening. This chapter asks why these questions are overlooked by improvers who try to stay uncontroversial. It looks at educational initiatives in various parts of the world which are more consciously political.

The third section *Learning* opens a discussion of issues which have been virtually neglected in the school improvement literature, despite their central relevance to raising expectations. Chapter 5 *Raising expectations – rethinking 'intelligence'* questions the assumptions behind our understanding of individual ability. It examines the history of intelligence testing and other practices and concepts which serve to deny the educational potential of working class and ethnic minority children, including theories of language deficit. It highlights the relevance for school improvement of newer models of ability, including the concepts of multiple and distributed intelligence.

Chapter 6 *Curriculum, class and culture* questions the rigidity of the imposed curriculum. It explores alternative models of curriculum in terms of their social values and political orientations. This chapter raises fundamental issues for educational achievement in inner-city schools, drawing on initiatives from the USA and Australia.

Chapter 7 *Pedagogies for improving schools* questions the emphasis on transmission models of direct teaching, and highlights the potential of recent developments in constructivist pedagogy. It draws upon research about classroom communications and thinking skills.

Chapter 8 *Schools for citizens* further develops the themes of curriculum, pedagogy and social power, and the relationship between education for citizenship and school improvement. It argues for opportunities to nego-tiate curriculum with young people, and to reconnect learning with action.

The fourth section, *Communities*, looks at the complex relationships between schools and their environments, and the contradictory support for social inclusion at national policy level. In much of the advice on school improvement, a one-way relationship is assumed between teachers and parents, and parental participation is limited to ensuring that children attend school and do their homework. Chapter 9 *Com-munities of learning* explores the social experience provided by schools, and examines the potential for real involvement of parents in the school and for learning in the community.

Chapter 10 *Social justice – or a discourse of deficit?* questions the neglect of a debate about social justice in mainstream School Improvement litera-ture. It re-examines the Improvement project in the light of theories of equity and inclusion, around a range of issues (poverty, special edu-cational needs, school exclusions, bilingualism, gender, racism and refugees) and emphasises the importance of overcoming discourses of deficit which ascribe problems to marginalised groups and individuals while leaving institutional structures intact.

The concluding section, *Futures*, has a single chapter: *Schools for a future.* It points to new directions for school improvement in the light of techno-logical and social change, developing understandings of teaching and learning, and an ethic of social justice and human rights.

CHAPTER ONE

School effectiveness: the problem of reductionism

> *Numbers are autocrats. They command belief. They impress us with their reality. They compel our respect.*
>
> (David Perkins, 1955: 41)
>
> *Everything counts, and nothing matters.*
>
> (Lord Northcliffe, at the start of the 20th century)

Research into school effectiveness has played a central role in setting the agenda for the improvement project in many parts of the English-speaking world. Although in common usage school *effectiveness* and *improvement* are often used interchangeably, the former is, strictly speaking, a statistical attempt to distinguish between more and less successful schools, using correlation techniques to identify reasons for success or failure. In its search for objectivity, it has distorted priorities for development towards outcomes which are most easily measured, placing overwhelming emphasis on test results as the desired goal. The impact of this research genre has been so serious that it is crucial to subject it to rigorous analysis.

A number of critics have pointed towards the reductionism of school effectiveness research. As far back as 1980, in a critique of Rutter's *Fifteen Thousand Hours*, Tony Burgess commented:

> My fear has been that managerial goals are being offered as a substitute for more fundamental debate about curriculum and pedagogy. (Burgess 1980: 13)

In the same volume, Hazel Francis pointed to its methodological simplification:

> It takes no account of the nature of the situation in which these variables are identified and measured . . . What we really want to know is how these

[variables] and the many others that we could think of, together with the
ecological variables we could identify, are interrelated for a particular
child, or for many, in a complex real-life fifteen thousand hours story.
(Francis 1980: 19–20)

This critique has re-surfaced periodically (e.g. Angus 1993; Grace 1995;
White and Barber, eds, 1997) and recently with increasing strength of
argument (Slee and Weiner, eds, 1998; Morley and Rassool 1999). The
aim of this chapter is to draw these arguments together in a systematic
way, setting them alongside statements from the principal defenders of
school effectiveness, in order to understand the problems with the
research paradigm and its impact on policy and practice.

Firstly, I wish to emphasise that I am not denying the existence of a
'school effect'. Even if claims are sometimes overstated, it seems indis-
putable that some schools achieve much greater success than others in
similar environments, in terms of examination success and of a wider
sense of achievement. More precisely, the problem lies in understanding
adequately:

• *what* counts as success

• *why* some schools achieve more of it

• *how* other schools can become more successful.

The term *school effectiveness* has been in use only since the 1970s, and in
Britain since around 1985; it has some international currency, partly due
to OECD projects, but not as much as is often claimed. It is only strongly
established in Britain, USA and the Netherlands, with firm roots in a few
other countries such as Australia, Taiwan and Hong Kong.

Whereas in German and French speaking countries, a quite broadly defined
concept of 'quality' is prominent, the Anglo-Saxon countries prefer the
narrower concept of 'effectiveness' which is empirically tangible but consequently limited to only a few of the effects of schooling. (Xaver Büeler,
1998: 666)

According to David Hopkins, probably Britain's most established school
improvement researcher, school effectiveness research shows:

• a pragmatic response to policy initiatives

• a commitment to quantitative methods

• a concern with the formal organisation of schools rather than with their
more informal processes

- a focus upon outcomes which were accepted as being a 'good' that was not to be questioned

- a focus upon description of schools as static, steady-state organisations generated by brief research study. (Hopkins 2001: 57)

By contrast, he suggests that the school improvement tradition has a bottom-up orientation, a qualitative research methodology, an emphasis on the dynamics of organisational processes, and a concern to 'treat educational outcomes as not *given* but problematic' (*ibid*: 56). Hopkins' distinction is helpful, though I have serious reservations about his final claim for School Improvement, which has itself been too ready to rely on test results as the prime outcome.

Biology, psychology and education

An interesting precedent for this evaluation of school effectiveness can be found in critiques by Steven Rose and colleagues of attempts to reduce psychology or sociology to biology or physical sciences. He argues that, although scientific method often makes tactical use of simplification (for example, when experimental method seeks to hold other factors constant in order to measure the relationship between a specific input factor and a chosen output) there are dangers if this is taken too far.

Reductionism is a belief that:

> events in high-level sciences can be reduced on the basis of a one-for-one correspondence to events and hence laws appropriate to the lower-level science. (H. and S. Rose, eds, 1976: 97)

That book, as also Rose, Kamin and Lewontin (1984), explores topics such as genetic determinism, intelligence testing, behaviourism, and 'biologism' (e.g. the belief that war is simply a manifestation of animal aggression). Building on their analyses, we can categorise some major aspects of reductionism which it is possible to apply to school effectiveness research:

  (i) a mechanistic causality, including a belief in one-to-one correspondences (which I have called *methodological* reductionism)
 (ii) a failure to examine environmental influences and effects when tracing causal relationships (*contextual* reductionism)

and in addition, a failure to question:

(iii) how ideas develop, and why they become popular at a particular time (*historical* reductionism)

(iv) the theory's social impact (*moral*, or political or teleological, reductionism).

An example: measuring 'intelligence'

These categories may become clearer for the subsequent discussion of school effectiveness by looking at Rose and colleagues' critique of how intelligence has been conceptualised as a single, measurable and innate capacity. Specifically, they examine the writings of Cyril Burt, the first British educational psychologist and the man responsible for applying 'intelligence tests' to select pupils for higher-level schools. (See also chapter 5 of this book.)

Methodological reductionism The concept of intelligence quotient (IQ) collapses a broad spectrum of abilities into a single quantity. Burt misappropriates the concept of physical capacity to argue that there must be fixed limits to what most children can learn:

> Capacity must obviously limit content. It is impossible for a pint jug to hold more than a pint of milk; [likewise] for a child's educational attainments to rise higher than his educable capacity permits. (Burt, in Rose *et al* 1984: 87)

Contextual reductionism Ability (quantified as IQ) is seen as innate and unaffected by learning. When Burt found that the children of Oxford University lecturers scored higher on intelligence tests than manual workers' children, he leapt to the conclusion that it had to be hereditary (*ibid*: 87).

Historical reductionism Burt's ideas were accepted uncritically at the time because they were politically expedient, while alternative notions of intelligence were ignored (see Chapter 5). His theory served to justify the retention of almost all working-class children in the elementary schools, where they received a cheap and inferior education until leaving school at 14. Only a few moved on to join more advantaged children in the grammar schools – a necessary exception in order to relieve a skills shortage after World War I. Flaws in his research reports were overlooked, and it was only after his death that his data turned out to be fictitious.

Moral reductionism Supposedly scientific methods help place policies beyond debate. They support the view that there is no point in giving working-class children an education which is supposedly beyond them because they've inherited low IQ? The common-sense of pseudo-scientific determinism held back the establishment of a more equitable system of comprehensive secondary schools – perhaps the most significant school improvement of the last half century.

School effectiveness: a reductionist paradigm

It may seem strange to compare school effectiveness research, which claims to be progressive, with the concept of innate intelligence, which certainly is not. Leading effectiveness researchers insist that their work is a way of overcoming a sociological determinism which makes working-class failure sound inevitable.

> We have convincingly helped to destroy the belief that schools can do nothing to change the society around them, and have also helped to destroy the myth that the influence of family background is so strong on children's development that children are unable to be affected by school. (Reynolds and Teddlie 2001: 103)

> In its commitment to maximising the educational quality of schools, both for its own merits and to generate wider social change, school effectiveness is the discipline in which radicals should situate themselves. (*ibid*: 111)

Unfortunately, this tends to sow the illusion of a freedom to succeed by educational effort alone, without challenging the structural inequalities in the social and economic order. Through its limited parameters, it helps to place out of bounds arguments about social inequality and prevents a more grounded examination of school failure.

Methodological confusion: what makes schools effective?

School effectiveness research (SER) attempts to mimic traditional models of natural science in establishing linear input-output relationships. This brings many problems of logic and methodology.

(a) Schooling has many outcomes, and there is no objective way of deciding which to focus on. SER veers towards measurable outcomes, and especially test scores. (Occasionally social outcomes are included, such as attendance or even, negatively, police arrests, but these are scarcely adequate indicators of social development.)

In Germany, there is an intensive debate about good and bad schools, but case studies are preferred to systematic empirical-analytical research. That is because we no longer see schools as mechanical input-output-systems but as complex social systems which are defined by processes rather than products. If you see holistic personal development as the aim of such systems, then school effectiveness analysis becomes rather difficult. (Büeler 1998: 669)

(b) Student development is affected by multiple factors within and beyond school which relate to each other in complex ways. A one-to-one causal link of inputs to outputs fails to represent the complex interrelationship and mutual reinforcement and interference of specific actions. Effectiveness studies typically conclude with a list of key characteristics of effective schools, with no explanation of how they interrelate. (Improvement research, on the other hand, prefers a less linear and more holistic study of the school *culture* as a nexus of meaningful actions and symbols – see Wrigley 2000: 27–30; Harris and Bennett, eds, 2001)

(c) It is a mistake to assume that statistical correlation amounts to causality. Only careful qualitative investigation within case study schools can establish which factors truly influence outcomes, rather than just being associated with them. (For this reason, effectiveness researchers often prefer the term 'key characteristics' to 'inputs', though in the end it amounts to the same thing within the logic of their argument.)

(d) School effectiveness research tries to distinguish 'malleable' factors (Scheerens 1998: 1099) which schools can control from those which they cannot, such as socio-economic factors. In reality, this is not so simple: attitudes, organisational choices and behaviours do not develop in a vacuum. School cultures are a 'product of the inter-action between the official culture of the school and the cultures of pupils' (Hatcher 1998: 280).

(e) Many factors are better seen as intermediate factors or process variables. On one level, good attendance is a necessary input – pupils who do not attend school are less likely to learn – but it is also an out-come: pupils are more likely to go to school if they enjoy the place and if they feel they are succeeding.

(f) Perhaps the greatest problem is the vagueness of the language used to define the key characteristics of effective schools. How do researchers decide that one school shows a 'clear focus on teaching and learning' but another does not – it is rarely a matter of yes or no, and what exactly do the words mean? Since the definitions are less exact than the calculations which follow, this undermines the reliability and validity of the mathematical calculations. Though it is not too hard to accept that weak leadership can create difficulties, we are left with the problem that 'strong leadership' can mean many different things, from supportive and inspiring to dictatorial. When the importance of assessment was identified in London primary schools in the late

1980s (Mortimore *et al* 1988: 223), this was to contrast those teachers who handed to the next year's teacher either a grade or examples of work, with others who provided no information at all to their colleagues. This distinction is worlds apart from the current obsession with data collection.

The looseness of terminology is hidden by the sense of certainty conferred by mathematical exactness. Though characteristics of effective schools are rarely capable of precise delineation, the appearance that they can be conveys the aura of scientific objectivity while simultaneously leaving them open to political reinterpretation and manipulation.

School effectiveness tends not to think too much about these problems. It has developed increasingly complex statistical methods, but assumes that a quantitative correlation can explain the dynamic interactions within schools and between schools and society.

However sophisticated the statistics, we are left wondering how it is possible to distinguish and apportion a wide range of characteristics to their consequences. How can one decide which of the numerous possible factors has a significant bearing on a school's effectiveness? In fact, the classic British study (Mortimore *et al* 1988: 248) acknowledged that the choice depends on professional judgement rather than any statistical objectivity. Likewise, when Sammons *et al* (1995) condensed the multitude of factors they derived from previous American and British studies into eleven key characteristics, they had to use professional judgement rather than some statistical method.

Recently, a leading Dutch effectiveness researcher has conceded many of these points:

> It is not easy to assess the exact empirical basis of the list of factors . . . Most reviews do not state the statistical significance nor the size of the effects of the various factors in terms of association with adjusted achievement results . . . The fact that numerous designs of school improvement projects have already taken these factors as a source of inspiration underlines that 'they appear to make sense' . . . The messages that we can draw from the school effectiveness literature are general orientations rather than very precise recommendations. (Scheerens 1998: 1110–3)

In complex systems, causes always appear in bundles, and only the presence of a whole series of conditions guarantees success. Linear thinking is not good enough: we need to think of causal networks, in which multiple factors make each other operational. (Büeler 1998: 672)

> The ultra-Darwinists' metaphysical concept of genes as hard, impenetrable and isolated units cannot be correct. Any individual gene can be expressed only against the background of the whole of the rest of the genome. Genes produce gene products which in turn influence other genes, switching them on and off, modulating their activity and function. (Rose, 1998: 215)

Finally, the hegemony of statistical forms of evaluation distorts what we mean by a worthwhile education; it robs the word *value* of its meaning as personal, social or cultural worth, reducing it to a monetary token, the exchange value of measurable outputs. It places important curricular questions beyond discussion; what children learn is seen as a given, and the teacher's role is merely to 'deliver' curriculum so that the impact of its transmission can be measured (more below).

Contextual reductionism: pushing the world to one side

No school is an island. School effectiveness research recognises this only tangentially and perversely, in its attempt to separate out the relative influence of home and school on attainment.

The relationship between a school and its environment is complex, dynamic and reciprocal. Some schools in high-poverty areas become more successful through an intelligent and hopeful engagement with the community; the school's improvement may sometimes even contribute to an area's economic regeneration. In other cases, school and community seem bound to each other in a downward spiral of helplessness and despair. Effectiveness research takes our attention away from the inter-relationship, since its methods involve statistically removing the environmental effects from the frame in order to concentrate on the 'school effect'.

> Family background, social class, any notion of context are typically regarded as 'noise', as 'outside background factors' which must be controlled for and then stripped away so that the researcher can concentrate on the important domain of 'school factors'. (Angus 1993: 361)
>
> Social class is reduced to a variable to be controlled for and thereafter ignored, rather than recognized as a vital element in terms of accounting for the level of measured effectiveness and strategies for school improvement. (Riddell *et al* 1998: 184)

When Teddlie and Reynolds (2001: 57) argue that effectiveness research does not 'ignore context variables', their choice of words simply confirms what is being denied – as if the communities which schools serve can be reduced to numerical data sets.

A wide range of problems are generated by this limited grasp of the relationship between school effectiveness and situational issues such as social class.

(i)   Having factored out the social context, the research typically concludes that schools can raise attainment by applying a neutral set of recommendations. In reality, the interaction of successful schools with their environments is problematic, and one which teachers and school leaders have to renegotiate on a daily basis. Successful multi-ethnic schools (Blair and Bourne 1998; Wrigley 2000) have qualities which are not captured by the generalised lists found in effectiveness research; they depend on cultural empathy, political sensitivity and a desire for social justice. These schools have a capacity to listen to the community voice, a curriculum which is inclusive towards community experience and traditions, and an ethos which is open and welcoming while challenging negative aspects of the street culture. Arguably, successful schools in adverse circumstances are effective precisely because they take the background fully on board. 'Turning around' a struggling inner-city school involves precisely that – turning around to connect and negotiate with the community and its circumstances, as opposed to building higher institutional walls.

(ii) School effectiveness research appears to be playing fair by accounting for background factors, but the cards remain stacked. By age 16, even the most effective schools with high poverty levels struggle hard to match the attainment of the least effective schools in more affluent areas (DfES 'Autumn Package'). Even value-added analysis does not correct this, as the impact of poverty is cumulative and the attainment gap grows substantially between age 11 and 16.

(iii) A few schools in poorer areas match or even outperform some less effective middle-class schools, but this does not alter the general trend, and it often serves as a pretext to blame the rest. Across the whole system, the attainment gap remains, correlating strongly with social class factors such as parental occupation, income and education. The high levels of dedication, time and effort and the exceptional leadership required to become a relatively effective school in an area of social deprivation are underestimated and unrewarded.

(iv) If the general level of attainment across an entire education system rises but the attainment gap between rich and poor areas stays as

wide, this does not help the poor. The currency of examination
results can become debased, and students from more disadvantaged
backgrounds remain as disadvantaged as before, despite rising exam
success.

Connecting with the community

As a school it sought to create a moral groundwork based upon internal
and external solidarity that would be worthy of the creative genius and
generosity of its students and constituent communities. For its founding
and organic connection was with its community – to involve, reflect, affirm
and develop it in whatever ways it could, particularly in its actional dimension. This means primarily that the school gives authority to its community,
it offers reason, involvement, dignity, solidarity and hope. (Searle 1997: xiii)

The support of parents has been won by reassuring them that their
children are in safe hands. After a theatre trip, Asian students are delivered
to the door. The parents come out, shake hands, invite the teachers in,
though this has to be declined in order to get the others home. (in Wrigley
2000: 87)

The previous head had refused to pay attention to important community
concerns and this had led to conflicts which were stirred up further by the
press . . . Now I think I've achieved a level of respect and I'm very honoured
to be invited to speak at the mosques. I had to listen a lot in the early days,
as there was a lot of anger and people needed to voice their concerns. (in
Wrigley 2000: 133)

Given the extent of misunderstandings, it is crucial that effectiveness
researchers should be outspoken in countering false conclusions. Sadly,
few have followed Peter Mortimore's example in speaking out publicly
against the illusion that greater school effectiveness can overcome
poverty on a broad scale. Mortimore has been a forthright critic of politicians' abuse of research to excuse the neglect of welfare, employment and
housing provision. (Mortimore and Whitty, 1997)

Historical reductionism: research in a vacuum?

In recent decades, scholars in many different fields have learnt the importance of professional self-awareness – of being conscious of their personal
perspectives and of the origins and current role of their disciplines. Since
Foucault, it is no longer possible to regard academic disciplines as fixed
entities floating outside time. Even in natural sciences, the current paradigm and the surrounding culture (not to mention cruder factors such

as sources of research funding) influence how research questions are framed.

School effectiveness research seems remarkably unaware of its own history. Its advocates generally see its origin as a reaction to the Coleman report (1966), as if this were merely a methodological turn. In fact the Coleman report, repeatedly disparaged for emphasising that social background has a far bigger effect than the differences between schools, was a groundbreaking document for the United States: it articulated what had been unmentionable: the impact of poverty and racial oppression on school attainment. School effectiveness research, by separating itself off from wider sociological studies to focus on the size of school effect, simultaneously deflected attention from the issues Coleman raised. Its conclusions – indeed the entire discourse which results from its chosen terms of reference – have comforted politicians intent on cutting welfare benefits.

School effectiveness research took off in Britain in the 1980s in the context of the Thatcher Government's marketisation of education (see Morley and Rassool 1999: 12–13; Rea and Weiner 1998: 22). The quasi-market and effectiveness research are mutually reinforcing: competition pressures headteachers to scan the literature for quick fix ways of raising attainment, and conversely the emphasis on statistical measures of success increases this competition by giving parents (as 'customers') misleading reasons for choosing one school over another. Effectiveness research has paid scant attention to the intense and unfair competition which actively *produces* failing schools. (A typical example, 'named and shamed' as one of the worst schools in Britain, was Rydings, in Halifax, an 11–16 'non-selective' school in a very poor de-industrialised area, surrounded by grammar schools, other schools with sixth forms and church schools operating covert forms of selection.) The term 'ineffective' implies that schools are autonomous units responsible for turning inputs into outputs by operationalising key characteristics. Angus called this:

> an isolationist, apolitical approach to education in which it is assumed that educational problems can be fixed by technical means and inequality can be managed within the walls of schools and classrooms provided that teachers and pupils follow 'correct' effective school procedures. (1993: 343)

Moral reductionism: schools without values

The positivism of effectiveness research is not just a methodological problem: it is intimately linked with the moral reductionism whereby researchers wash their hands of responsibility for the social impact of their work. Lauder, Jamieson and Wikely (1998) refer to an 'abstracted empiricism' which ignores 'cultural, political and historical questions'. The academic discourse leads its researchers to see themselves as objective and scientific and thereby absolved from moral judgements.

Here the gatekeepers of the effectiveness paradigm condemn themselves from their own mouths, openly insisting upon acquiescence with dominant political forces.

> The 'narrow agenda' of pragmatists working in SER is more realistic at this point in time than the 'redistributive policies' of the critical theorists . . . Pragmatists, working within the SER paradigm, believe that efforts to alter the existing relationship between social class and student achievement by bringing about broad societal changes are *naïve, perhaps quixotic*. We prefer to work *within the constraints of the current social order*. (Teddlie and Reynolds 2001: 70–71, my italics)

They fail to ask: progress towards what? Like other scientists researching nuclear fusion or genetic engineering, they wash their hands of any responsibility for the application of their research – the defence of Pilate. (*ibid*: 2001: 51) This is disingenuous given the intimate relationship, especially in the UK, between their research and its government sponsors. Stephen Ball (1998: 73) rightly speaks of 'Faustian deal-making between the academic and politicians'.

Researchers have to rely on funding from official bodies, but there is a loss of integrity if they do not speak out against the misuse of their findings, which are often channelled via media soundbites into moral panics and then by government into quick fix initiatives.

With some honourable exceptions, there has been a failure to acknowledge the adverse consequences of the effectiveness research and discourse:

- that highly visible comparisons between school results affect teacher supply and thus damage the effectiveness of many schools in poorer areas

- that accountability, assessment and target-setting marginalise parts of the curriculum which are less easily measured, such as the humanities and the arts. (See OISE/UT 2001 and HMI 2001 for an account of how high-profile testing in literacy and numeracy is squeezing out other studies in primary schools)

In its rare engagement with more successful schools in areas of depriva-tion, effectiveness research has tended to praise those which reduce the curriculum to basic skills instruction (e.g. Teddlie and Stringfield 1993; Hallinger and Murphy 1986). Literacy is of vital importance, but needs to be developed within a meaningful and lively curriculum. The Accelerated Schools network (see Meier 1998; Levin 1998) is a reaction against the practice of consigning many poor and minority students to a curriculum of tedious decontextualised exercises. These schools, along-side intensive teaching of key skills, deliberately engage with higher-level cognitive challenges which connect with the students' lives. This project, involving over a thousand schools in the USA and rigorously evaluated, receives the barest mention in the *International Handbook of School Effectiveness Research* (Teddlie and Reynolds 2000), which instead high-lights some small-scale research praising schools with a restricted curri-culum. It appears that the school effectiveness paradigm is not simply a methodological specialism in Raymond Williams' sense, but a 'selective tradition'.

Reductionism and political reaction

The relationship between reductionism and political conservatism is complex. It would be wrong to suggest that effectiveness researchers have deliberately set out to produce a reactionary discourse; in fact, many operate from a genuine concern to improve educational opportunities for disadvantaged students. It is rather the paradigm, the discourse and the associated set of practices which steer the research in particular directions.

This chapter is certainly not intended as a general attack on statistical studies. The problem is, more precisely, that effectiveness research is limited by working in one direction. This is acknowledged by three well established effectiveness researchers from the Netherlands, who define it specifically as an attempt to correlate outcome variables with 'malleable school and classroom conditions' to explain school differences after 'adjusting for student intake characteristics' (Scheerens, Bosker and Creemers 2001: 132). The privileging of 'school effect' distorts the picture by systematically pushing other factors into the distance. In effect, it regards the background factors as 'assigned conditions' – an unalterable fact of life.

The very same techniques favoured by school effectiveness research can also be used in the opposite direction. Instead of factoring out socio-economic factors as a fixed background, research can also highlight these factors precisely because they *are* politically changeable if there is the clarity and the will to tackle them. A key example is Gillborn and Mirza's (2000) influential study of the relative importance of class, race and gender in the UK. This demonstrates, among other things, (a) that the attainment gap between professionals and manual workers' children has grown; (b) that African Caribbean children leave school with the worst qualifications despite being more advanced when they enter; and (c) that there are places where this problem has been overcome. Bruce Biddle (1997) uses statistical modelling to challenge the USA's funding system which reinforces disadvantage; he shows how poverty compounded by poor funding in the poorest school districts is largely responsible for the relatively low attainment in the USA. Jürgen Baumert and colleagues at the Max Planck Institute in Berlin expertly use regression analysis to demonstrate the injustice and ineffectiveness of a selective school system (Deutsches PISA-Konsortium 2001; summarised in Baumert and Schümer 2002).

Such studies, along with statistical research relating to linguistic and cultural diversity, is totally sidelined by the gatekeepers of School Effectiveness. The 400-page *International Handbook of School Effectiveness Research* (Teddlie and Reynolds 2000) presents a selected canon, neglecting for example the rich and extensive studies on the impact of bilingual education (cf. Cummins 2000: 247, summarising studies such as August and Hakuta 1997). It becomes clear, from scrutinising such contrary examples of statistical studies, that School Effectiveness is a paradigm which is defining itself ideologically as well as methodologically.

> Children of ten and younger have developed an ability to speak two languages fluently, moving in and out of each from one minute to the next . . . A Pakistani child who accompanies her mother to the DSS and translates into Punjabi for her, unravelling the massive social inequality within the complex bureaucratic wordmaze of her second language, and bringing it into meaning and sometimes additional benefits for her mother: what a testing! Yet what reward or recognition, beyond a service of love – while a middle-class child of the suburbs gets an 'A' in a 'modern language' like French or German, which she learns dutifully through books and teachers but rarely speaks or uses in any organic, life-centred way. So what is achievement: is it the banking of passive fact by an individual learner, or the use and application of living experience in the service of others and the struggle to develop your own community? (Searle 1997: 2)

The terms in which the whole field is framed tend to sow illusions that increased efforts by teachers will result in greater social justice. We have a modern version of the Victorian ideology of the 'self-made man':

> Any capitalist there, who had made sixty thousand pounds out of six-
> pence, always professed to wonder why the sixty thousand nearest Hands
> didn't each make sixty thousand pounds out of sixpence, and more or less
> reproached them everyone for not accomplishing the little feat. What I did
> you can do. Why don't you go and do it? (Dickens: *Hard Times*, 1854)

Effectiveness researchers are inevitably affected by a political and cultural
environment in which financial values predominate over human ones.
The dominant discourse is that of economic rationalism whose tacit
purpose is concealed by the non-discussion of educational aims. Lingard,
Ludwig and Luke (1998) relate economic rationalism in education (the
replacement of a values discussion by one about performance and
efficiency) to the wider moral reductionism within capitalist economy
and culture:

> Economism recognises no other form of interest than that which capital-
> ism has produced, through a kind of real operation of abstraction, by set-
> ting up a universe of relations between man and man based, as Marx says,
> on 'callous cash payment' . . . (originally Bourdieu 1990: 112)

The postmodernist denial that any shared 'Enlightenment' values are
possible, the extinction of any 'grand narrative', the fragmentation of a
public values discourse, has merely served to reinforce the power of the
raw cash nexus of a society which remains *late capitalist* rather than *post-*
something.

By contrast, Gerald Grace (1998: 120–4) appeals for a 'values-added'
inquiry, not just 'value-added' research. He argues that it is no use just
talking of effectiveness and schools making a difference – we must
ask: difference to what? He speaks of a 'mission reductionism' which is
particularly uncomfortable for the Catholic schools he has researched.

But the reductionist paradigm and discourse of school effectiveness does
not merely *derive* from the ideology of the wider society. Through its discursive closure to debates about educational and social values, it actively
reinforces the hegemony of economism by placing essential issues out of
bounds.

The result is a hegemonic version of School Improvement which concerns itself with the management of change irrespective of where that
change might lead.

An alternative model of school development can be built by analogy with the development histories of other living systems, and described in ecological rather than linear terms:

- The evolution of living systems is self-organising and dynamic (i.e. not simply the result of causes but of a long and accident-prone learning history on the system-environment border)

- Developments can only be sustained if they have an equilibrium between innovation, verification and preservation

- Development takes place through exchange effects, more exactly, through the synchronisation of processes on the macro and micro levels. (Schools must connect effects on a personal and social plane. School development involves personal, social and organisational learning.)

- The evolution comes about through a reciprocal interplay of biological psychic and social development actions. (Learning processes are necessarily holistic – head, heart and hand. If you ignore this, you end up with medium- and long-term damage to personal development.) (Büeler 1998: 675)

CHAPTER TWO

School improvement: where do we go from here?

> *Effective schooling and the school improvement movement is blind to a searching interrogation of outcome. Test scores become ends . . . Explicit discussions of values and the types of society to which schools articulate/ adhere are ignored.*
>
> (Slee and Weiner, 1998: 111)

Part of the problem with words like 'effectiveness' and 'improvement' is that no one could possibly disagree. To ask an audience of headteachers whether they would like to improve their schools is like asking them whether they are in favour of personal hygiene or being kind to animals.

This is precisely the reason why we need to examine the use of words which, through their seepage into everyday common sense, have so successfully pervaded our public space. The demand that we improve or become more effective discursively underpins the operations of an entire education system. We are looking at a discourse, or rather a *discursive practice* which connects research, policy, and administration to a degree which has begun to exclude alternative ways of thinking.

Words develop meanings in particular historical and social contexts. We need to explore the specific meaning which 'improvement' is acquiring today, and particularly in England, whose education system is virtually a testbed for a particular model of educational change.

Thinking seriously about educational aims is a reflective process involving historical, psychological, social and philosophical understanding. It is many years since Harold Silver raised the issue of what we mean by 'a good school'? We cannot make sense of improvement unless we can decide what *better* means.

> Good schools have . . . trained girls to be good wives and mothers or . . .
> boys to serve the commercial ethic or the Empire. Good has been an
> infinitely adaptable epithet, used of schools of many kinds by interested
> parties of many kinds. (in Riley and MacBeath 1998)

We need to interrogate such obvious words as *achievement*, digging below
the surface of taken-for-granted meanings. Ofsted (the inspection agency
for England and Wales) distinguished between the words achievement
and attainment, defining the latter as the subset of achievement which
could be tested. This helpfully served to acknowledge that many worthwhile achievements could not be measured. Unhelpfully, of course,
Ofsted privileged the attainments while marginalising other kinds of
achievement.

A few years ago, I tried to articulate a broad but situated concept of
achievement' for bilingual communities such as the young Pakistani
Muslims I had worked with in Rochdale, England:

> We need young people who are skilled tabla players and computer users,
> who enjoy Asian films and Western books, who are able to lead themselves
> and their communities forward through change and storm and a calm sea,
> who are socially aware and morally committed and no one's fool. We need
> a very wide definition of achievement. (Wrigley 1997)

This is not to underestimate the importance of exam success: ethnic
minority school leavers desperately need certificates as testimony to their
intelligence and potential in the face of racist assumptions which still permeate our culture. Similarly, teenagers growing up in poverty on housing
schemes need formal qualifications to overcome the prejudice of employers who shortlist by postcode.

Academic qualifications are crucial, but they are not enough. In fact, one
of the conclusions I reached during the fieldwork for *The Power To Learn*
(Wrigley 2000) was that schools serving marginalised communities
cannot raise attainment without promoting and celebrating achievement
in the widest sense. Besides, without a broader personal, social and
cultural development, the working class or minority youngster would go
out into the world unable to deal with its challenges.

School improvement – a contradictory development

Substantial advances have been made since 1990 in understanding the
processes by which schools improve. From early mechanistic attempts to
apply a list of key characteristics of effective schools or generate tick lists
of managerial actions, a more organic understanding of process has

developed. In its exploration of school culture, distributed leadership, complexity theory and school self-evaluation, School Improvement is infinitely more illuminating than ten years ago. There are however some key problems which we need to face up to.

According to David Hopkins (2001: 56) School Improvement distinguishes itself from School Effectiveness through:

- a 'bottom-up' orientation in which improvement is owned by the individual school and its staff

- a qualitative orientation to research methodology

- a concern with changing organisational processes rather than the outcomes of the school

- a concern to treat educational outcomes as not 'given' but problematic

- a concern to see schools as dynamic institutions requiring extended study more than 'snapshop' cross sectional studies.

Much depends on the fourth of these points. In his editorial introduction to a section of the *International Handbook of Educational Change*, Hopkins defines school improvement as follows:

> a distinct approach to educational change that enhances student outcomes as well as strengthening the school's capacity for managing change. (1998: 1036)

Hopkins may have intended a broad definition of 'outcomes'. The problem is that a narrower definition so permeates educational policy at the present time that, in the absence of an explicit challenge, 'student outcomes' is inevitably understood in terms of basic skills and examination grades. If this is all we mean by outcomes, then school improvement is trapped within the limited purposes of school effectiveness; and simply adding the term 'capacity for managing change' compounds rather than removes the problem.

This problem permeates so much of the current literature on school improvement. Experienced writers in the field unwittingly fall back on language which suggests a narrow set of aims, such as the argument that more autocratic leadership has largely failed to 'deliver instructional improvement', 'focus upon the improvement of instruction and student performance' and 'improve student learning outcomes' (Harris 2002: 2).

(I deliberately cite Alma Harris and David Hopkins in this chapter, as two of the most influential and experienced leaders within the field of School Improvement in England, and researchers to whom we owe a great deal. If we climb on the shoulders of giants, we can see that much further.)

We cannot develop our understanding of the school improvement project without reference to the wider political situation. Helen Gunter (2001: 19) contrasts 'the neo-liberal version of the performing school' with 'the performing school [which is] concerned with the ideas and practice of democracy'.

In the former:

> Education is a product and service to be marketed, bought and sold, as the most efficient and effective way of organising and meeting consumer needs. The purposes of schools and schooling are to enable the workforce to be appropriately skilled to operate in the current and developing economy.

whereas in the latter:

> Education is a public good, it is an entitlement and promotes equity. The purposes of schools and schooling are to educate as well as train, and to enable children to engage in the theory and practice of what it means to be a citizen in an unfolding and reforming democracy project.

While much of the school improvement literature acknowledges the limiting characteristics of the neo-liberal environment, it significantly fails to challenge them. Structural problems such as greater central control, the punitive regime of inspections, marketisation and the illusion of the quick fix are sometimes mentioned in the early pages of a text and then forgotten.

Hopkins (2001: 21–24) provides a theoretical key to understanding the tensions within school improvement by drawing upon Habermas' model of the 'three ways in which humans know and construe the world' (Aoki's adaptation) – the *technical, practical* and *emancipatory*.

(i) An empirical-analytic (technical) orientation has an interest in efficiency, certainty and predictability; understands in terms of facts; and seeks technical control of the world. (Though Hopkins associates this with a 'short term' school improvement focus 'using bureaucratic policy options and narrow outcome measures', it also fits the school effectiveness paradigm.)

(ii) A situational interpretative orientation attempts to understand the social world in terms of the meanings people give to situations, of authentic intersubjective understanding. Reality is 'inter-subjectively constituted' and explanation involves 'striking a resonant chord by clarifying motives, common meanings and authentic experiences'. (Hopkins correctly identifies this with recent trends in school improvement, a focus on process and culture.)

(iii) Finally, a critical orientation seeks to improve the human condition by uncovering 'tacit assumptions' and initiating a liberating process of transformation.

It is here that Hopkins' conclusion becomes most questionable. He locates as (iii) school improvement which is 'authentic', which emphasises 'student learning, intervention and empowerment'. Such a vague definition really does not provide a sound foundation for building a socially-critical version of school improvement, which, in Habermas' model, would require us to think beyond the frame of common sense assumptions by scrutinising the political interests behind an hegemonic view of reality.

Helen Gunter (2001: 73) argues that 'transformational leadership', in its current usage, is not really transformational. She cites Gerald Grace's argument (1995) that 'the current model of charismatic transformational leadership lacks the necessary radicalism needed to pursue issues of equity' (Gunter 2001: 41). Transformational change would entail a challenge to the role of schooling in reproducing the unjust power structures of our world. This would require us to rethink curriculum, pedagogies and the undemocratic relationships and structures in which pupils are socialised. The dominant trend in the school improvement literature is to stop short of such a political challenge, though there are some signs that we may now be edging towards a paradigm shift.

Distributed leadership

In *The Power to Learn*, I emphasised the importance of shared leadership.

> This is not to imply that the headteacher is unimportant. In all these schools, the head has played a determining role in making the school what it is today. It is simply that many other individuals have also played important leadership roles, and the success must be attributed to all the players . . . It is vital to effective school development that the relationships and structures encourage the emergence and practice of leadership and creativity in different quarters. (Wrigley 2000: 159–161)

There has recently been increasing focus on this concept, a development which Alma Harris and others are currently taking forward under the rubric of 'distributed leadership'. This is seen as inherently democratic, challenging the 'dualism of leader and led' (Harris 2002: 3).

> Distributed leadership therefore means multiple sources of guidance and
> direction, following the contours of expertise in an organisation, made
> coherent through a common culture. (Harris 2002: 4 citing Elmore)

We need to question the concept more critically or it will underachieve
on its democratic potential. When we study quotations from some of the
headteachers cited in this same paper, we see how easy it is to slide into a
different interpretation:

> To be confident in your own ability to delegate tasks and know they will be
> done . . . to allow people to lead and not to try and control everything your-
> self.

> You set the way forward, lead by example, communicate what needs to be
> done and have to be hands on in the way you want it achieved . . . it doesn't
> always have to be you doing the leading.

This is precisely the problem identified by writers such as Helen Gunter:

> Shared leadership is functionally downwards. It is about getting teaching
> and learning done, measured and made visible in externally determined
> ways . . . Middle management [is] responsibility shifted down the line . . .
> within the school. (Gunter 2001: 111 summarising Grace 1995)

> Opportunities to lead have traditionally been in the gift of the headteacher
> as a 'leader of leaders' (Day 1995: 126) . . . The distribution of work has
> been conceptualised on the premise of avoiding potential headteacher
> overload. Increasingly the neo-Taylorist approach to getting new tasks
> done efficiently and effectively has been given a new-wave gloss in which
> delegation is the means through which individuals in teams can learn and
> develop. (Gunter 2001: 131)

She goes so far as to suggest that even headteachers have become more
like middle managers, despite the promises of empowerment through
delegated management:

> The mandated models of school leadership . . . are not about educational
> leadership but about enabling the leadership to be a middle manager to
> both implement and be accountable for centrally directed policy . . . Edu-
> cationalists and communities were sold site-based performance manage-
> ment on the grounds that it would enable more participation to identify
> and meet local needs, and yet local priorities have had to take a back seat
> while centrally determined agendas have been implemented. (ibid: 148–9)

Meanwhile, teachers are being proletarianized through 'the separation of
design from implementation combined with work intensification' (ibid:
145) while being engaged in a spurious collegiality.

The neo-liberal version of the performing school requires teachers and students to be followers, but to feel good about it . . . Teachers talk about 'pseudo participation' where views are sought as a ritual rather than a sincere attempt to listen and take note . . . Development planning is more about allocating tasks and responsibility than it is about asking questions about how and why things are what they are, and how they have come to be. (*ibid*: 122–3)

The problems of the education system have been laid at the door of teachers while their capacity for findings solutions has been taken away. The rhetoric has been of empowerment, participation and teams, but the reality is that teachers have had to continue to do what they have always done – be empowered to do what they have been told to do. (Gunter 2001: 144)

This is precisely the form of 'contrived collegiality' identified by Andy Hargreaves (1994), where the agenda is always set by powerful others. That is why we need to engage in a philosophical analysis of key terms, and a critical engagement informed by clarity of purpose.

> Theorising about power enables us to engage in discussions about influence, authority, dependency, manipulation, resistance, support, interests and legitimacy. (*ibid*: 136)

Schools are storehouses of distributed knowledge; it frequently governs the micropolitics of the organization . . . The collective memory of this institution is located everywhere in it; there is, then, a need for careful storage, access to, and retrieval of this collective memory. This respects the person-centredness of schools; all the participants in the school can make a knowledge contribution to the school; leadership equates with dispersed, distributed leadership . . . The notion of distributed intelligence and information has huge implications, for it argues against hierarchical and bureacratic command-and-control approaches to management and leadership and, instead, argues for the realization that systems are more fittingly conceived to be networks (just as the brain is a series of neural networks) – loosely coupled or more tightly coupled. (Morrison 2002: 19)

In particular, teachers need to reassert their right to debate the purposes of education. Shared leadership, in a fully democratic sense, is more than mere delegation; it involves a range of voices being heard, perspectives being shared, conflicting interpretations of reality debated. It involves not only participating in finding the solutions, but in having a right to argue about what is the problem. Above all else, successful distributed leadership in inner city schools means giving voice to those who originate from, or have an understanding of, the local communities and who are engaged in making curriculum meaningful to students. It is a form of distributed cognition (see Perkins 1992) in which the combined experience and awareness adds up to more than the parts, and diverse perspectives are needed to lead development.

Finally, leadership, at all levels, must be based on moral and political values. This means rather more than just a dedication to higher standards and improving school ethos; it has to engage with social justice and the real-life dilemmas facing the students. In successful multiethnic schools, Maud Blair and colleagues (1998) found headteachers and others who:

- gave a strong and determined lead on equal opportunities

- empathised with the political and social factors which affected the lives of their students

- listened to and learnt from students and their parents

- tried to see things from the students' point of view

- created careful links with local communities.

Understanding school cultures

One of the greatest advances in school improvement research has been the focus on school cultures.

> School cultures . . . are dynamic and created through the interactions of people. They are a nexus of shared norms and values that express how people make sense of the organization in which they work and the other people with whom they work.

> Although powerfully visible through various symbolic processes, organizational culture is often taken for granted by current participants in an organization who may be unaware how a particular culture has been constructed, how it might or can be changed or how it is sustained by those people in positions of power and authority. (Busher 2001: 76)

> The culture of an organization, then, is a construct made up of a range of expectations about what are proper and appropriate actions . . . This raises two very important questions . . . where the expectations that define legitimate action come from and how they become part of the assumptive worlds of each organizational member. (Bennett 2001: 107–9)

School cultures are highly contested. School improvement cannot be understood by focusing on internal processes alone but require us to look at the interaction between internal and external cultures. The dominant ideas and values within the wider society, the principles which permeate the macro-political culture, are not only transmitted downwards through a management hierarchy, but permeate our general consciousness as discourse, thus entering into our assumptive worlds.

There is, within each school, a contest of different voices, which is what makes school development so interesting. Indeed, it is this that makes school development *possible*. The voice of teachers who insist upon challenging inequality, tedium, and superficial or irrelevant learning is a powerful force for change, despite attempts to silence it. The voice of the local community, carried by staff (teachers and assistants) who are in tune with its problems and aspirations, is crucial to the successful development of multiethnic and other urban schools.

Youth cultures are often seen as an obstacle to school achievement, and may have this effect. It is certainly true that a commercial culture framed by instant gratification and bought pleasures makes young people impatient with school learning. At the same time, we cannot simply turn our backs. (Paradoxically, as Jane Kenway reminded the ICSEI Conference, Toronto 2001, the same corporate forces which are culturing children as consumers are turning schools into 'pleasure-free zones' through high-stakes testing, an imposed curriculum and transmission teaching.)

The conflicts that arise from the gap between dominant school cultures, on the one hand, and the crises of children growing up in poverty, dealing with racism or the life choices offered by mass media, on the other, can lead to a dysfunctional disengagement of adolescents from learning. The challenge for school improvers is to find creative ways of engaging with the various cultures and interests at work, and to develop a learning culture which supports achievement and social development within this context.

It is time for school improvement research to develop a more contextual and critical sense of the dynamism and contradictions of culture formation in schools. Whereas the dominant version sees cultural leadership as an homogenising force, effectively co-opting teachers into the government's view of successful schooling, creative and responsive school development requires a vision forged out of the many voices of staff, students and communities. The monocultural version of the good school has not proved very helpful in the inner-city or in the outer-ring housing schemes.

It's a myth that parents don't care about their children's education. They do, but often they don't know how to engage with it. We have had to take the initiative and make extra efforts to be accessible. We've worked with other agencies to run family literacy projects. We've persuaded the community centre to put on workshops to help parents help their children. We've recently been talking about targeting 20 year olds, older brothers and sisters who were once our students, and are therefore better placed than their parents to help the current students.

We don't tolerate a macho street culture. We've established a pride in the school . . . This hasn't meant cutting ourselves off from the real world. In fact, our school values are very close to the values of the home, and particularly the Asian communities. We draw on that kinship-based value system. Our set of values is really very simple: respect, family and achievement. (Linda Woolley, headteacher, in Wrigley 2000: 88)

School improvement requires a more political and situated exploration of culture than we have managed so far, and specifically in relation to demands for greater democracy and the achievement of real success in inner city schools. For example:

- exploring the differences between authoritarian and cooperative cultures, including developing new rituals for cooperative and democratic learning (see Petersen 2001)

- examining the cultural significance of alienated forms of learning, in which, like factory work, you are told what to write and then hand over your product not to an interested audience but to the teacher-as-examiner, for token payment in the form of a mark or grade

- questioning the culture of target setting and surveillance which regulates the lives of pupils and teachers, and exploring more democratic forms of educational responsibility than the present accountability culture

- examining the cultural messages of classrooms which are dominated by the teacher's voice, closed questions and rituals of transmission of superior wisdom

- developing a better understanding of cultural difference, in order to prevent high levels of exclusion

- understanding how assumptions about ability and intelligence are worked out in classroom interactions

- discovering how assumptions about single parents, ethnic minorities and 'dysfunctional' working-class families operate symbolically in classroom interactions.

These issues are developed in later chapters.

School improvement, democracy and social justice

School improvement, as a research paradigm, policy mode, and set of practices, did not develop in a vacuum or simply from the good intentions of dedicated teachers. Its recent emergence can be located within a political configuration involving:

- demands for greater competitiveness within a global market
- the marketisation – and increasingly, privatisation – of schooling
- the development of a 'disciplinary' regime (inspections, performance pay etc) which harnesses teachers to government-sanctioned views of curriculum and social development
- politicians' need to blame teachers and 'failing schools' rather than admit their own failure to reduce child poverty.

School Improvement, at least in its officially sanctioned forms, has had a number of profoundly anti-democratic effects, which can only be touched on here. It is important to recognise them, so that they can be challenged more forcefully.

A growing attainment gap

The attempt to make schools in poorer areas more effective by skilful management of internal change, while failing to challenge the macro-environment (competitive admissions, creeping selection, imposed curricula, judgemental forms of assessment) has led to an increased attainment gap between different social groups. The gap is apparent when children enter school, and substantial by the end of primary school, but grows during adolescence to the extent that hardly any schools in poorer areas even touch the national average level of examination success at age 16. In fact, of the secondary schools where 35 per cent or more pupils are entitled to free school meals, only 2 per cent reach national average examination results at age 16 (Ofsted 2000; see also Gillborn and Mirza 2000; Mortimore and Whitty 1997; Levacic and Woods 2002).

Accountability and surveillance

A profound transformation is underway in professional culture, reducing teachers' individual and collective control over their work. This change, though brought about in the name of 'democracy' (responsibility to parents who are seen as customers rather than partners in their children's education), actually serves to hinder teachers from working more democratically with students and parents. The terms of 'accountability' – to whom, for what, on which criteria? – are far from democratically determined, and education is increasingly made to serve the needs of globalised capital (Burbules and Torres, eds, 2000).

The performativity culture leads to thoughtless knee-jerk responses to external demands for change which are inimical to authentic and sustainable school improvement.

> Progress is defined in terms of outputs which strip away the sense of improvement of the human condition in favour of material and technical growth. (Clarke 2001: 29)

Teachers are denied teleological influence and moral responsibility. They inhabit a 'technically rational' system which denies 'any sense of historical consciousness as having a bearing and a relevance upon school life' (*ibid*: 29).

Limited space for responsiveness and initiative

The cultural patterns of British schools derive historically from the repressive traditions of the Victorian age, established as much to domesticate the children of the poor as to teach them the 3Rs. They have been modified over the years by teachers and school leaders brave enough to develop new forms of learning and relationship. In a fast moving world, it is vital to maintain an openness to change in schools. Reinforcing the shortcomings of inherited patterns, the increasing regulation of school norms represents a regressive and undemocratic closure.

For all the talk of a 'postmodern' age of uncertainties and the need to accept rapid change, attempts persist to define teaching in terms of a technical-rationalist list of sub-skills graduated for different career stages as competences. This is a reversion to a Fordist mass-production model of quality assurance which is at odds with the wider culture we inhabit and serves to make teachers feel forever inadequate.

Management of professional actions by set formulae is even more difficult given the social and cultural instabilities of the surrounding culture and the need to respond creatively to children whose identities are structured around the immediate gratification of consumer pleasures – or even worse, the tensions for those who lack the money to buy these pleasures. Spontaneity is driven out, along with human emotion. Teachers are expected to record every detail of advanced planning and obsessively record outcomes. There is a neglect of the professional quality of responsiveness, thinking on your feet and dealing with the unexpected. This particularly affects teachers working in the most troubled schools.

The emotional commitment of teachers is being sapped, and intensification of work, the guilt of not doing anything properly and a lost sense of moral purpose, is leading to the collapse of professional morale. In this climate, the attempt to impose positive emotions works in highly contradictory ways:

> The neo-liberal version of the performing school requires teachers and students to be followers, but to feel good about it . . . As Nias (1996: 305) argues, teacher emotion 'is not an indulgence; it is a professional necessity. Without feeling, without the freedom to 'face themselves', to be whole persons in the classroom, they implode, explode . . . or walk away. (Gunter 2001: 122)

Teacher demoralisation and shortages

The demoralisation resulting from a 'low-trust high-surveillance' regime (Mahony and Hextall 2000) is corrosive of commitment, and such a culture quickly proves its unsustainability. Seemingly, the politicians' only answer is yet another set of targets.

The most visible impact of this high-pressure performativity culture has been a major recruitment crisis, such that nearly half of new teachers qualifying in England now leave within their first two years, and overall one in ten teachers leave the profession each year. The crisis has particularly hit those schools which have always found the greatest difficulty attracting teachers.

> In order to achieve improvement, such schools have to exceed what could be termed 'normal' efforts. Members of staff have to be more committed and work harder than their peers elsewhere. What is more, they have to maintain the effort so as to sustain the improvement. (Mortimore and Whitty 1997: 6)

In an environment of high-stakes accountability, schools in poorer areas have become dangerous places for teachers' careers. Results are lower in absolute terms, and progress between two points in time is less. Performance-related pay discriminates against teachers in these schools. They are emotionally more stressful, and their pupils are less likely to respond to longer-term goals and pleas to work hard. Despite the official use of 'value-addedness' and more sophisticated comparisons with roughly similar schools, it is raw results which remain visible in local and national newspapers. Inner-city schools are at far greater risk of being named and shamed as 'failing' – always the common expression, despite the official euphemism 'schools in special measures'. The cure is a tough regime to 'turn them round' (Ofsted 1999) – a fallacious strategy which often further demoralises, and does not help a school to rethink itself as an educational institution in relationship with a community. Finally, schools in poorer areas are faced with high-profile threats of closure and privatisation from government ministers.

Superficial responses to government initiatives

The Literacy Hour for English primary schools is a prime example. While some teachers struggle to interpret it in the light of more advanced professional knowledge, the majority are driven by insecurity to implement it mechanistically as a set of regulations to spend twenty minutes on this and ten on that. Consequently, alongside good methods such as collective thinking about texts and building children's self-image as readers, there has been a return to decontextualised exercises which do not transfer into real literacy skills. Ironically, whereas the DfEE advised in 1997 that everybody should be 'working to the same blueprint', and the Literacy Strategy's director warned those opting for alternatives that they would be 'interrogated' (sic!), the Inspectorate now appear to be criticising teachers for a lack of creativity.

Five and six year old children are being labelled inferior readers and given restricted reading experiences. Training videos have encouraged a return to the pseudo dialogue of closed testing questions, rather than genuine response and discussion of books. The traditional asymmetry of classroom communications is reinforced – the hidden curriculum by which children learn that their voices do not count. Teachers' anxiety about the tests is getting in the way of their ability to respond to the concerns and interests of young readers.

When you're doing reading and writing with year 6 [10–11-year-olds] you've always got your eye on what they have to do for their SATs, so you're asking questions like, can you spot the personification in this poem, or can you find a simile or use a simile in your writing. You're just picking out the main things that you think they're going to be asked about. (Year 6 teacher, in Hunt 2001: 55)

The drive for more transmission teaching

When the National Curriculum was first introduced, teachers were advised that they would be told what to teach but not how to teach it. Since then, there has been increasing pressure on teachers to use approved methods, and especially whole-class direct instruction. The emphasis on teaching as transmission positions students as passive, obedient and dependent.

International tests which identified Taiwan as a high achiever in mathematics led to the inspection body Ofsted sending a well-known effectiveness researcher to investigate. Not surprisingly, he found much whole-class instruction – that was the clear intention of the mission. However, subsequent video-recordings comparing maths teaching in Japan with the USA have found a deeper pattern. Stigler and Hiebert (1999) have linked Japan's high performance to higher levels of conceptual understanding. Japanese children are set challenging problems to solve collaboratively in groups, whereas American students are instructed in procedures which they then have to practice individually.

Teaching in England is now under the influence of performance pay, based on flawed private research which has been exposed by the British Educational Research Association (BERA 2001). Close scrutiny of the research shows only a random correlation between the recommended teaching style (based on Reynolds' criteria) and good progress: only 55 per cent of the teachers who were deemed outstanding according to the approved criteria achieved better than expected results, and half the classes with above average progress were taught using different methods. Despite this, the DfEE has disseminated these supposed criteria of effective teaching skills for schools to use as a standard observational tool for evaluating teachers.

An antidemocratic curriculum: limiting social understanding

The National Curriculum in England and Wales, on its first introduction, modernised teaching in the technical and scientific domain (an extended science curriculum; the design and technology reform; a high profile for information technology) but seriously restricted learning about the contemporary world. Now that education for citizenship has been introduced, we will need to ensure that it isn't undermined by mindframes of accountability. Already multiple choice tests are being introduced by examination boards, which may serve to trivialise learning. Official guidelines to teachers classify three different levels of social understanding in the most absurd manner:

At the end of this unit

most pupils: understand what it is to be an active citizen with rights and responsibilities.

some pupils have not made so much progress and: understand in simple terms what rights and responsibilities are.

some pupils have progressed further and: use the terms 'right', 'responsibilities' and 'community' with confidence and accuracy.

Issues such as poverty, racism, globalisation are marginalised, distorted and trivialised when treated in this way:

At the end of this unit, most pupils understand their own identities and recognise that there are many different identities locally and nationally. (QCA 2001)

Meanwhile history and geography are crowded out of the primary school curriculum by the 'basic skills'. For increasing numbers of 14-year-olds, instead of developing more relevant content and methods, schools are encouraged to replace a balanced curriculum by vocational training.

Unfortunately, school improvement is discussed in Britain as if the curriculum does not matter very much. A genuine desire to improve schools would take seriously the needs of young people who are growing up in a world that is ecologically fragile, military threatened, and globally dominated by a small number of very rich individuals/businesses, and in which values and relationships are shifting so uncertainly.

Moving forward

My aim in this chapter was to examine the limitations and contradictions of a dominant version of school improvement in the particular situation of Britain. School Improvement stands at a crossroads. On the one hand, some voices seek to co-opt it as a subset of School Effectiveness or call for a merger between Effectiveness and Improvement. More positively, a number of British writers are moving onto more critical and democratic enquiries, often in fruitful cooperation with Canadian or Scandinavian colleagues. For example:

• John MacBeath (1999; 2000; 2003), working closely with Jean Rudduck and with European researchers such as Michael Schratz, is seeking to democratise change by focusing on school self-evaluation, including the involvement of students as researchers of their own schools (the Student Voice project)

- Keith Morrison (2002), influenced by Senge and Perkins, is using complexity theory and distributed cognition as a means of understanding school development

- Louise Stoll, Dean Fink and Lorna Earl (2003) have connected learning by students, professional learning and leadership into a vision of the learning school

- A more rigorous theoretical exploration is taking place of school structures and cultures (Harris and Bennett, eds, 2001) and of the concept of leadership (e.g. Gunter 2001)

We need now to move forward with hopeful determination. Those who are seeking to make schools better and more powerful sites for education need to engage in philosophical debate about educational aims and values, curriculum and pedagogy. This necessarily involves thinking about the kind of world we hope to live in. We need a new direction for improvement, one which is not so dependent, which can focus on social justice and responsibility and global citizenship, which is future oriented and genuinely transformational. We need to engage in an active search for new models of *democratic* learning, not sit blindfolded on the conveyor belt of 'effective' schooling.

CHAPTER THREE

Commitment or surveillance: the ecology of change

> *In healthy systems there is sharing and networking of good practice within and among schools on a collegial basis. It is an unhealthy system which relies on the constant routine attentions of an external body to police its schools . . . In such a system there is an important role for an Inspectorate or Office of Standards: to make itself as redundant as possible.*
>
> (John MacBeath 1999: 1)

Improving a school is a journey of hope based on shared beliefs and values and real commitment. Michael Fullan has consistently written of school leaders working with their colleagues to build a vision for the future – a message enthusiastically adopted in numerous schools around the world.

By contrast, teachers in England in particular have been subjected to an extraordinary drive to control schools from above. The mechanisms and language of 'accountability' are everywhere, corroding educational processes, and affecting teachers and students alike.

The 'high surveillance, low trust' described by Mahoney and Hextall (2000: 102) is not an ecology of sustainable development. It is profoundly demotivating, and a direct contributor to teacher shortages. It undermines the daily dynamics of teaching, which depend as much on emotions and flexible responsiveness as rational planning, and destroys the trust on which lasting improvement depends.

It is also subversive of the community building which is a necessity in any serious school improvement effort (Sergiovanni 1994: xi). Sergiovanni writes of a Californian school:

> In their self-driven research processes, participants came to openly discuss their hopes and dreams. Through this process, we understood there were

shared common values around which we could begin to imagine a more ideal school. (*ibid*: 21).

This is the most essential difference between changes driven from within and without. Self-evaluation is intimately linked with the desire to improve; external evaluation which is imposed from above leads to a mess of conflicting emotions. We know that even when school inspections go well and the school gets a positive report, the staff are often left burdened and exhausted. Far from leading to improvement, research in England has shown that examination results dip in the summer after a school is inspected (Cullingford 1999). When the inspection goes badly, schools are left in a morass of negative feelings.

Authentic sustainable change requires a climate of trust.

> Without trust, people divert their energy into self-protection and away from learning. When trust is lacking, people will not take the risks necessary to move the school forward. When distrust pervades a school culture, it is unlikely that the school will be an energetic, motivating place. Instead a culture of self-preservation and isolation is likely to pervade the school. (Mitchell and Sackney 2000: 49)

Without that trust, teachers are in no position to care for their students, and the environment is too fragile for fruitful change:

A great deal is said in the school improvement literature about a positive ethos and high expectations. When teachers feel badly about themselves, how can they make their students feel well about themselves?

A regime that provides human beings with no deep reasons to care for one another cannot long preserve its legitimacy. (Richard Sennett 1998: 148)

Accountability or responsibility

Fred Inglis draws a sharp distinction:

> 'Accountability' is, after all, not the same thing as responsibility, still less duty. It is a pistol loaded with blame to be fired at the heads of those who cannot answer charges. (1989: 35–54)

Drawing on this thought, Michael Fielding (2001c) argues that accountability 'tends to operate in hierarchical regimes . . . Motivation tends to be extrinsic to the task in hand and the sustainability of the required work rate or specified outcomes has more to do with the threat of penalties than the fulfilment of internal satisfaction or moral obligation.' Such accountability is profoundly undemocratic, and quite different from a genuine sense of responsibility to an identifiable community, but the concept has become reified, so that we no longer ask why or to whom we are accountable.

It undermines teacher professionalism, by always placing them in a position of deficit to externally-set targets which they can never hope to meet. Jamieson and Wikely (2001: 172) argue that this model of accountability derives from the world of mass production as in the early American car factories, and is deeply alien to educational environments:

> It is tempting to see a shadowy Tayloristic model in some of the school-effectiveness writing. There are 'experts' who have discovered the best way of teaching certain subjects; it is 'science' (cf. Reynolds' 'applied science of teaching') and the 'workers' are to be instructed in these new models.

Management experts such as Senge now argue that this is not a good way to manage a commercial enterprise; it is truly ironic, at a time when industrial management consultants are drawing upon complexity theory, that government agencies are trying to impose an archaic and mechanistic model of linear rationality on schools. But there are deeper problems in trying to manage schools this way. The central processes of education are undermined by language that doesn't articulate moral purpose (Fullan 1993). The discourse of performativity, of efficiently fulfilling specific targets, is deeply corrosive of education. Fielding, in a critique of the language of SMART targets, argues:

> Overemphasis on what works (in this case the raising of test scores) forces prior questions of purpose, i.e. what test scores are for, from the centre to the periphery of our attention and, in so doing, runs the risk of marginalising education in favour of a more limited notion of schooling. (Fielding 1999)

The more specific the government is about what it is that schools are to achieve, the more likely it is to get it, but the less likely it is to mean anything. (Reay and Wiliam 1999)

Caged birds don't fly

'You can't mandate what matters. The more complex the change, the less you can force it.' Michael Fullan's aphorism is pertinent but not strong enough, as the accountability regime for English schools is actively undermining even what is already established.

> I tell you what I am finding tricky at the moment . . . it has to be an ever deepening sense of loss of time . . . I feel so tired all of the time and just seem to be chasing shadows . . . its effect is to gnaw away at self-confidence . . . never enough time for us to stop and think as a team about what this initiative or that initiative means . . . we just do it . . .

> It is a sense of loss as well . . . we feel like we have lost the closeness that we really value here . . . I feel ashamed really . . . I'm harassing people I've worked really closely with for five years to conform because their performance threshold depends on it.

> The climate has shifted . . . it is all so damn serious now . . . lots of suits . . . grey-suit reform . . . I feel *compromised*. (Headteachers interviewed by Paul Clarke 2001: 26–27)

This disruption of time, of relationships, of trust, ethic and ethos, is ultimately the manufacture of despair.

> I think it undermines our professionalism particularly when it comes to being told what we can or can't do with our students here . . . I can put up with most things in this job but I fear for my colleagues who are disillusioned . . . good teachers who are reporting to their team leaders a sense of despair at the scale of the demands they face . . . they are saying that they don't have time to build reasonable relationships with the students . . .

> They don't have the fun with students that they used to . . . they feel more detached and isolated from the curriculum they are teaching . . . give us the book and we'll teach it is something I'm hearing more and more of but I know that it is a cry of despair. (*ibid*: 28)

This concern is shared by Michael Fielding, who questions whether teachers can give proper attention to young children when they are constantly under pressure of external demands:

> How many teachers, particularly those of younger children, are now able to listen openly, attentively, and in a non-instrumental, exploratory way to their children/students without feeling guilty, stressed or vaguely uncomfortable about the absence of criteria or the insistence of a target tugging at their sleeves. (1999: 280)

Emotions are central to teaching, not an optional extra, so a loss of authenticity or emotional integrity totally undermines our relationships and actions. Inglis warns against the *instrumentality* brought about by constant quality control:

> The preposterous edifice of auditing, the mad rout of acronyms – HEFCE, TQM, OFSTED, TTA – blinds vision and stifles thought. Their most

certain consequence is to make enquiry service, knowledge instrumental and, above all, to make all of us, teachers at whatever level, boring, exhausted and hating the job. (Inglis 2000: 428)

Sustainable school improvement depends on a sense of hope and authentic purpose. As Paul Clarke argues, the current performativity regime is destroying teachers' orientation towards the future; it produces a 'sinister seriousness' which 'is eroding the identity of the teacher as a caring professional and replacing it with a functional technician . . . The fragmentation of the teaching process through target setting, combined with the depreciation of value as a currency of meaning inside the system, leads to alienation, lack of concern for each other as people and loss of any sense of sustainable self.' (Clarke 2001: 30–31)

It is important for teachers and heads to speak out, and to articulate their experience and analysis of this environment, but more, to engage together in a collective resistance to the mechanisms of the accountability regime. Academics concerned for school improvement would do well to support the development of a collective voice – this would make a more significant contribution to sustainable improvement than collusion with the accountability regime.

Collective action and pressure were sufficient, for a while, to prevent tests being run and to delay the introduction of performance-related pay in England. In Scotland, the idea of performance bonuses was rejected in favour of an enhanced pay scale linked to study towards a Masters degree. Teacher unions in Canada and Australia are engaged in debates and active resistance to such destructive regimes. In the USA, teachers and academics have organised in the collective Rethinking Schools to campaign against government policy and at the same time to publish resources for socially-critical learning.

However, it is right to demand that politicians and officials should waken up to the limitations of the present regime. The caged bird cannot fly – or at least, not far.

Opening the cage

What can be done to resist and undermine the present accountability regime and to replace it with practices of responsive evaluation which are more democratic and build on the principle of hope? What are the issues and possible strategies?

Motivation

It is possible to establish checks to establish a minimum level of quality such as 'maximizing time on task' and 'keeping accurate records of pupil progress', but this will never be enough to lead to high achievement. High reliability checks may be OK for McDonalds, but student motivation is what really counts in schools. Teachers too will be better motivated if they are able to reclaim their creativity in curriculum development, and to engage in some negotiation about content and methods with the students.

Risk-taking

The confidence to take risks is vital in a changing environment. Learning from the Jackson-Keller School in San Antonio, Sergiovanni (1994: 173) says risk-taking involves:

• Going beyond the 'norm' and being open to new ideas

• Fear and excitement at the same time

• Assuming responsibility – flexibility – reaching new heights

• Going out on a limb with a safety net and being allowed to fall

• Going beyond what you feel you can do

• Believing in yourself

• 'Going for it'

• Doing things you haven't done before, falling out of your mould, not getting stale

• Gambling to go beyond mediocrity

• Trying new methods/approaches – being able to accept the consequences.

Keeping an eye on the big picture

In a high-surveillance regime, 'The push is more for the specific, the detailed, and the obvious. Slowly . . . we begin to lose the ability to focus on the moral, aesthetic, existential and intellectual dimensions of learning to live inside communities of people.' (Inglis 2000: 30) Teaching is more than a set of discrete competences which lead to a 'drab utilitarian view of schooling'. Teachers work cannot be 'calibrated . . . pre-defined in accordance with requirements which circumscribe the degrees of choice and decision-making within which they operate'. (Mahoney and Hextall 2000: 90)

Thinking skills need thinking teachers

Narrow attempts to direct teachers can only achieve restricted types of learning:

> There is evidence that technicist approaches based on a behaviourist view of learning promote some basic skills and raise tests scores. This narrow and shallow perspective on teaching and learning, however, contributes little to pupils' desire to imagine, create, appreciate, and think critically. (Fink 2001: 232)

Build the capacity for self-evaluation

Low-trust regimes are very expensive to administer.

> The 'conventional wisdom', propagated by the popular press, corporate leaders, and ambitious politicians, is that teachers and other educators are the source of most problems. They must, therefore, be obliged to comply with mandates through elaborate and usually expensive accountability measures. (*ibid*: 231)

Dean Fink also points out that the very states (North Carolina and especially Texas) which British officials have used as exemplary models are those where the testing tail wags the teaching and learning dog and where the system discriminates heavily against the least advantaged.

Share higher-level aims

Bureaucratic measures lead to a tokenistic fulfilment. Teachers change 'just enough to avoid sanction. Change stops when sanctions are moved.' Even in schools which depend on personal loyalty to a strong leader, without a shared vision teachers change 'just enough to receive gratification of needs' (Sergiovanni 1998: 580). The energetic pursuit of worthwhile goals requires a genuinely collegial environment.

Focus on values

Competences don't discriminate between formal and real fulfilment. A 'trainer' for NPQH, the main English headteacher qualification, argues:

> The big questions aren't dealt with at all in the Standards – what if the candidate is a Nazi? I've got a woman at the moment and she's not a nice person . . . she shouldn't be there. I wouldn't want her near my child. She's horrible. She can't stand kids . . . but there's nothing in the NPQH Standards that says you have to like kids or care about them – or other human beings come to that. (Mahoney and Hextall 2000: 54)

Develop a broad view of quality indicators

The competences discourse is so widespread that it is essential to look at the alternatives. The *Standard for Headship in Scotland* (SEED 1998), for example, sandwiches broad descriptors of professional actions' between values and personal qualities. The new *Standard for Chartered Teachers* (SEED 2002) examines the contribution of the experienced professional in terms of broadly defined areas of commitment, rather than a list of competences; the supporting examples are illustrative rather than prescriptive. It places great importance on educational and social values, and on teachers as reflective practitioners. The word *effective* is used to refer to more than just attainment: it entails promoting students' personal and social development, and facilitating the learning of children who are facing difficulties. (This definition of advanced professionalism was not, of course, achieved without the foresight and determination of the academics and teachers who drew up the key document, and their refusal to be drawn down the performativity road.)

Publicly challenge the accountability regime

Michael Fielding (2001a) uses the sub-title *Four Years Hard Labour* for his outstanding book on New Labour's educational policies in England and Wales. The previous government's mechanisms of control and surveillance have been extended and tightened, so the struggle to dismantle them will not be easy. A monolithic system has been established in which professional requirements established by the Teacher Training Agency are disseminated by the Standards Unit of the DfES and policed by Ofsted. This body now inspects everyone from toddlers to directors of education – a monolithic surveillance from cradle to grave. This means, however, that more people have a stake in dismantling it!

Expose the inadequacy of the 'quick-fix' solution

Government agencies are still laying down quick-fix top-down methods for improving struggling schools, such as Ofsted's recipe for 'turning round' schools in special measures:

- *strong* leadership
- *vigorous* action to improve the quality of teaching, pupils' progress and levels of attainment *quickly*
- and taking steps *quickly and effectively* to improve pupils' behaviour.

Let us focus instead on providing sustainable and non-threatening support for schools in difficulties.

Rebuild initial teacher education

The system is seriously damaging the education of new teachers. One headteacher commented on the new competences:

> We need professionals not technicians, thinking and reflective intellects not insensitive bullish practitioners, flexible, developmental learning providers and not routine, systems-orientated instructors . . . Unless they (teachers) can inspire the young people they teach as well as instruct or direct them, they will end up as . . . the teaching version of Mr Plod. (Mahoney and Hextall 2000: 45)

Teacher educators, and their mentors in schools, need to reassert the need to consider issues such as democracy, social justice, curriculum design and personal and social development. These are professional rights and responsibilities, not an optional extra. Beginner teachers need encouragement to see themselves as reflective practitioners from the start.

Models of responsible professionalism

Self-evaluation

We have to argue for processes which promote genuine responsibility rather than its parody 'accountability'. Internally-driven school review has been shown to work in many different education systems. John MacBeath successfully promoted the idea of school self-evaluation, which is officially embedded in the Scottish system through the document *How Good is Our School?* There is always a danger of complacency, but schools are beginning to use critical friends and consultants, including local authority advisers, to avoid this.

The three principles of successful evaluation

(i) Self-evaluation must have priority. It is much more effective for school development than external evaluations, and should therefore be the starting point of any evaluation process.

(ii) External evaluation is necessary, because the internal participants inevitably have their blindspots. (External evaluation may include standardised tests or a formal inspection, but invited consultants, peer reviews from colleagues in other schools, and observation by academics or parents might be more useful.)

(iii) Authentic evaluation must be distinguished from 'façade evaluations'. Façade evaluations are most likely when they are imposed from without, or when there is no agreement between internal and external actors, or when it is felt to be threatening. (Rolff 1998: 31)

John MacBeath's recent books (1999; MacBeath, Schratz, Meuret and Jakobsen 2000; MacBeath and McGlynn 2002) provide accounts of many different approaches to self-evaluation, including an entire 'toolkit' to support different activities.

Networks

In the United States, many schools have engaged in voluntary networks such as the League of Professional Schools, the Coalition of Essential Schools and Accelerated Schools Project (see References for websites). Often these bodies unite around principles which run counter to official policy or traditional practices. Members agree to the central aims of the coalition, but are free to find their own solutions. For example, the Coalition of Essential Schools seeks to develop challenge and in-depth learning rather than wide curriculum coverage. It believes in establishing smaller communities within larger schools, each with a team of responsible teachers who can cover the major specialisms between them – and no teacher to be involved with more than 80–90 pupils in total. The organisation provides conferences and on-line communities for sharing ideas, as well as support through resources and with evaluation.

Parents

We cannot and should not go back to a principle of full professional autonomy. The world has changed, and other professions such as doctors have had to adjust to an increasingly vocal and informed client group.

It is claimed that professionals who are opposed to accountability are simply refusing to be responsible to the public who finance the service. (The bizarre accusation of 'provider capture' implies that teachers want to dominate education for their own ends.) We need to insist on establishing genuine responsibility to a visible community, rather than to remote government bodies and their agents. Jorunn Møller (Norway) emphasises the importance of defending standards and values by engaging in open discussion with parents:

> Principals and teachers should enter the public debate with both their critiques of educational policies and their internally defined criteria of teacher professionalism. A professional role entails professional responsibility, and this implies that teachers and schools leaders must make their experience more visible and public. (2002: 18–19)

This involves real debate, including a struggle for values:

> Education's responsibilities are primarily to the democracy of *citizens* rather than to the democracy of *consumers*. (*ibid*: 19)

Student voice

Finally, we need to develop new ways of recognising student rights. John MacBeath and Kate Myers are coordinating a project *Consulting Pupils about Teaching and Learning* which involves learners researching their own schools. The students are involved in framing the research questions, and not only in providing or gathering information. The findings then feed into school development planning. (See the special issue of *Forum* on *Student Voice*, Fielding 2001b.) The most exciting and ambitious project has been the *Learning School* project involving students from eight different countries in evaluating their own and each others' schools (MacBeath and Sugimine 2003).

Michael Schratz (Innsbruck) has developed a new approach to consulting young children on school development. Recognising the imbalance of power when adults interview children, he gave children cameras to take a set of photographs which they displayed and discussed with each other and their teachers (in MacBeath *et al* 2000: 151). Another method is to ask pupils to keep a diary (*ibid*: 153).

Other models of learner involvement are being promoted by the Scottish School Ethos Network (see website), through the enhanced use of school councils and the promotion of student-run initiatives. The network organises an annual conference and produces regular school reports.

Changing conceptions of leadership

One of the most misleading declarations of school effectiveness research is that schools need 'strong leadership'. (The choice of adjective was not, however, decided by the statistics; it was a category chosen by the researchers, starting in the late 1980s – and it is worth noting that leadership and management were barely mentioned in Michael Rutter's (1979) famous study *Fifteen Thousand Hours*.) The word *strong* is capable of a range of meaning. It might reflect determination in protecting colleagues from bureaucratic overload or less important government initiatives; it might mean enabling staff to reinterpret them to fit local needs; it may involve skill and sensitivity in changing the attitudes of more cynical teachers. Government agencies which sought out 'superheads' who could 'turn schools round' found the formula of little practical value when many of those recruited proved ineffective in the situation or resigned. The nature of headship clearly depends upon our view of educational purposes and the particular context.

Given the serious difficulties of school development in areas of high poverty and migration, it is remarkable how few qualitative studies have been undertaken. There is the beginning of a body of evidence which indicates that the improvement of inner city schools requires a strong values base, including social justice and a willingness to engage with community perspectives. (Blair and Bourne 1998; Wrigley 2000)

Often headteachers derive meaning and motivation from their own roots. I interviewed Carol Howarth, head of Spittal Primary School in Glasgow, a school with a mainly white working-class population and high levels of poverty:

> I get very angry when people write off working class communities, partly because that's the background I'm from. My parents were keen that all of us gained qualifications, and it upsets me to hear people talk as if parents in an area don't care about education. (Wrigley 2001: 17).

Tom MacDonald, head of All Saints High School, Glasgow, has spoken to the media many times about the positive impact of asylum seekers on his school. He clearly identifies with their situation not only from a Catholic perspective on social justice but also from his own family roots:

> We have had families removed in the middle of the night to the Detention Centre at Dungavel, people who suffered terribly in their home countries. But we should also question the words *economic migrant*. My own family were economic migrants from Ireland. It's about survival, not greed, and a natural desire for a decent life. And many Scots left for the USA and Canada as economic migrants. (Wrigley 2002: 4)

'High expectations' for his school is a political concept, involving dimensions of personal effort and international solidarity:

> It's not 'how clever are you?' but 'how are you clever?' If you're clever at organising a disco, we value that, and you can move from one area of success to another . . .

> We emphasise at assembly that it is our *privilege* to help our International Students, and that we can learn a lot from them – about the world, about different ways of living, and about other people's problems. And it's about the gospel values of caring for one another, of being a community where people care for each other. (*ibid*)

Reva Klein interviewed a Hackney primary head 'of Italian parentage, married to a Turkish Cypriot, speaking with an unmistakeable Belfast twang. No wonder she's rapturously at home with parents from the four corners of the world.' There is clearly an autobiographical element in her determination to provide an exciting education for her diverse community, and to 'get away from drumming things into the children according to the National Curriculum' (Klein 2001: 3).

The responsiveness and rootedness of school leaders has received far too little attention in official documents and in research. In explaining the qualities of an *intelligent school*, and consequently of intelligent leadership, Barbara MacGilchrist lists contextual intelligence, reflective intelligence, collegial intelligence, emotional intelligence, spiritual intelligence, and ethical intelligence. These are aspects which we should continue to explore for schools in particular contexts.

- Contextual intelligence . . . is characterised by a welcoming responsiveness to visitors, new ideas and events in the immediate environment.

- Collegial intelligence describes the capacity for staff in particular to work together to improve their practice in the classroom . . . Underpinning collegial intelligence is a recognition that whilst individuals can make a difference, the sum of the parts is greater than the whole when staff work together to improve and develop one another's practice.

- Emotional intelligence is to do with a school's capacity to allow the feelings of both pupils and staff to be owned, expressed and respected. (MacGilchrist 1997: 104-8)

Shared leadership in context

There is increasing interest in the distribution of leadership in schools (see Chapter 2 above). This may require structural as well as cultural changes, in order to enable teachers to work together. Its success also depends on thoughtful evaluation of the ways in which power is shared.

The distribution of power and influence is context dependent. A particular feature of successful schools with bilingual students is leadership from the English as an Additional Language specialists, including discussion of whole-school policy, observing lessons from the learner's perspective and coaching colleagues in the classroom when introducing new teaching methods (Wrigley 2000). This cannot happen successfully if the language specialists are simply peripatetic visitors, floating between schools and unable to develop a sufficient level of trust. It also requires serious professional development for the EAL teacher, through extended courses and regular cooperation with similar specialists working in other schools. Similarly there is considerable untapped potential for development of the leadership role of learning support and pastoral/guidance staff in other types of school.

A major dilemma for new headteachers is the balance between personal leadership and developing the leadership of others. Fullan insists that it is insufficient to speak of conveying or sharing a vision, there must be collective vision-building. However, new headteachers often find some resistance to these more democratic expectations.

> Some people quite frankly said, 'Look, it's the principal's job to make decisions' and almost accused me of abdicating my position. I explained to teachers that I don't have a monopoly on good ideas. (Blase 1995: 107)

This is clearly a difficult tension to negotiate, requiring flexibility and compromise alongside conceptual clarity. Sergiovanni accepts that a new principal, faced with a lack of consensus on goals, may have to begin by relying on *bureaucratic authority* ('position power, the authority of rules, the control one has over rewards and punishments') and *personal authority* ('in the form of human relations skills – to enter into a series of trades with teachers'). This might be necessary to 'get enough unity in what we are doing, enough common effort, to begin a meaningful dialogue' (1994: 194). It is important to be clear from the start, though, on the need for community building.

This involves building a community life involving staff, students and parents, and moving towards a shared purpose, a strong sense of collegiality, collaboration and professional community. Roles are no longer so sharply differentiated: 'Let kids be leaders – let teachers be learners'. (1994: 171) Sergiovanni argues that his ideal of a community of leaders is not impossible:

> In communities leadership is not defined as the exercise of power over others. Instead it is the exercise of wit and will, principle and passion, time and talent, and purpose and power in a way that allows the group to increase the likelihood that shared goals will be accomplished. (*ibid*: 170)

Sergiovanni is critical of styles of 'personal leadership' which take the form of people-handling skills. His preferred focus is on shared meanings:

> Leaders rely less on their people-handling skills and more on the power of compelling ideas and the meanings they hold for others.

Cultures and values – the wider environment

School improvement research, along with the practical efforts to develop schools, is focusing increasingly on the transformation of school culture, but there is a temptation to concentrate on the internal dynamics within schools as if this could be separated from the wider context. In reality, school culture and development is closely bound up with the wider environment, both in terms of the school's locality and in terms of political policies.

Authentic school improvement, in a context of accountability and top-down control, is a problematic activity. Shared leadership and collegiality are necessary in order to resist some of the pressures, but they require ideological clarity about the wider environment.

In a blame culture, it is helpful to remember Bourdieu's advice that, even though it is painful to make social suffering visible and to theorise the connections with the power structures, it is also 'liberating for those who had thought it was all their fault' (Bourdieu 1999: 629).

Teachers and principals who wish to turn their schools round need to begin by turning themselves around to engage with the life experiences of the families they serve. They need to reconnect education to the life of the community, however difficult this may seem.

Clarity is the beginning of resistance. School leaders need to defend their educational values against an adverse wider culture. *Leading Schools in Times of Change* (Day *et al* 2000) shows how headteachers need skill in resolving tensions and dilemmas in ways which do not leave them compromised. Their leadership depends on the cultivation of hope, in themselves and in their schools:

> In mediating between their own moral framework and those of the communities in which they worked, their focus was always upon the betterment of the young people and staff who worked in their schools. They remained also, often against all the odds, enthusiastic and committed to learning. Their strength was demonstrated in their hopefulness at all times. (*ibid*: 178)

CHAPTER FOUR

Whose improvement? whose schools?

> *The achievement of the highest socioeconomic groups is very similar in different countries, but the achievement of the lowest groups is radically different. The highest achieving countries have the smallest spread. The way to raise standards overall is to concentrate on raising the achievement of the poorest sections of society.*
>
> (Professor Jürgen Baumert, director of the Max Planck Institute of Educational Research, Berlin, following analysis of the PISA study)

School improvement does not take place in a vacuum. The internal development of schools relates to wider social and economic change. The purpose of schooling, its funding and governance, is defined in terms of a variety of economic and social goals. Students come from and return to a wider environment.

It is understandable that much of the early school improvement literature chose to concentrate on the internal change process, but this now seems profoundly limiting. A few historical examples might illustrate the importance of a contextual understanding of improvement.

Educational change depends on perceptions of wider social needs. In a divided and hierarchical society, the most powerful class in a society has a powerful influence; at the very least, it can set the outer limits for change. The need of the dominant class to safeguard its position of power often conflicts with the need for technical development.

In Britain, writers on school improvement and effectiveness have generally fought shy of relating educational change to wider social and political change. In the few books which appear to promise a more historical understanding, the explanations tend to be apolitical. Thus the 1988 Education Reform Act might be explained in terms of a demand for better value for money following the economic recession of the 1970s (without saying which sections of society were making that demand) but

- Hannah Moore launched her literacy campaign during a period of great political reaction. (The Duke of Wellington was fighting the remnants of the French Revolution in Europe, and breaking the Luddite risings at home.) She determined to teach the poor how to read, i.e. religious tracts advocating political restraint and obedience, but refused to allow them to learn to write in case they chose to express their grievances and organise politically.

- Universal full-time schooling after 1870 was intended to provide basic literacy and numeracy skills but also to domesticate the children of the industrial working class and keep them in order. Voting rights had just been extended, so a form of elementary schooling was introduced which would socialise the poor into subservience. The government cynically declared 'We need to educate our masters'.

- The adult education system in nineteenth century industrial towns was begun by skilled workers. They opened Mechanics Institutes, run by workers themselves, with lectures on science and technology, history and politics. Local industrialists and church ministers rushed to sponsor them and take them over, reducing the curriculum to scientific and technical matters.

- Throughout the Victorian period, girls were taught sewing and cooking in preparation for their role as housewives and domestic servants – even in areas where most women worked in textile mills. For most of the 20th Century, practical teaching for boys was based on the slavish reproduction of set designs determined by the teacher. Until the Design and Technology reform, archaic wood- and metalwork were taught; this was dysfunctional in terms of current industrial needs but helped to socialise future workers by inculcating order and obedience.

with no reference to the Thatcherite political reaction and its dramatic effect on education. At that time, the Conservative government, as part of a broad attack on trade unions and other centres of resistance, abolished the Inner London Education Authority – a pioneering body that had led the way in educational development by helping teachers design a more relevant curriculum and improve teaching, as well as focusing on social justice and equality. Throughout England and Wales, local councils' powers were reduced so that they could no longer allocate extra support to schools in most need. Headteachers were offered a limited form of autonomy, the hidden price being subjection to a centrally imposed curriculum and assessment, and control through league tables and inspections. Parents became consumers and teachers were to be turned into obedient transmitters of inert knowledge.

School Improvement grew up in this environment, offering explanations which largely overlooked curriculum, pedagogy and equity, and fighting shy of political explanation. It now requires courage to reinsert School Improvement into the political narrative, and to warn against government policies which are undermining the basis of improvements so far achieved.

The comprehensive school reform

The escalating attack by New Labour politicians on the very principle of comprehensive schools is a matter of central importance for school improvement. In just over a year, policy has shifted rapidly: first, a leading government press officer releases a soundbite disparaging 'bog standard' comprehensives; then the education minister outlines her five new categories of secondary school, an entire caste system of 'comprehensives' (or should we call them 'post-comprehensives'?) and finally the Prime Minister speaks about the supposed failure of the comprehensive system.

The same government which has kept curriculum in a straitjacket and imposed on primary schools a uniform method of teaching literacy, now has the nerve to promote its post-comprehensive hierarchy under the slogan of 'diversity'. It denies that this is a return to a selective system, but cannot explain how they will prevent it. The specialist schools are allowed to select a proportion of pupils – a percentage which will undoubtedly grow. How exactly will the 'specialist schools' and 'advanced specialist schools' divine a ten-year-old's potential in business or Chinese? In truth, it will simply open up new routes for some parents to use their influence and cultural capital to negotiate advantage for their children.

Advocates of school improvement cannot cut themselves off from this political debate. It would be hypocritical to speak of raising expectations and transforming school culture while systems are created which will condemn an underclass of children to an underclass of schools. Concerns for the internal processes of school development cannot be divorced from an interest in structural reform.

The comprehensive system in Britain has been enormously successful in raising achievement. It has opened up to the majority of children an education previously reserved for a few. In 1960, 20 per cent of children were selected for grammar schools, and 16 per cent of 16-year-olds passed five O-levels. In 2000, in a system which was still mainly comprehensive, 50 per cent achieved the equivalent five GCSEs at A*–C grades. In 1970, 47 per cent left school with no qualifications; now only a few percent do so (Tomlinson 2002). In Scotland, where all state secondary schools are comprehensive, recent research shows that middle class children (defined as having fathers in professional occupations and parents who stayed at school to age 17 or beyond) gain equally good exam results in state schools as in independent schools (Paterson 2002).

If the comprehensive system is a failure, the 2000 PISA study certainly doesn't show it. PISA is the first major international study to survey children of an identical age, rather than those taught together within a particular school year group. (Previous studies such as TIMSS were distorted by countries such as Germany where large numbers of lower-achieving pupils are kept behind to repeat a class, or countries where large numbers placed in special schools were not included in the survey.) In PISA, Britain's 15-year-olds scored high in all three assessed subjects, literacy, mathematics and science. Almost all the high-achieving countries have comprehensive systems to at least age 15, and in some of the highest, internal divisions such as streaming and setting are illegal. The overall pattern is for higher achieving countries to have a low spread of attainment. (The unusual feature, in Britain's case, is the wide spread of attainment, which, as in the USA, can be attributed to the extent of poverty.)

In Germany, by contrast, a system with three tiers of secondary school has proved disastrous. (Comprehensive schools exist in parts of Germany, but usually alongside and in competition with the other schools, rather than including all pupils in a town. There is, in addition, also a fourth layer, the special schools.) Germany had at least expected that children attending the Gymnasium (the highest level, or grammar school) would achieve very highly, even if many in the Hauptschule (the lowest level, or secondary modern) were struggling. In fact, at both ends of the scale, Germany's results are a cause for alarm: there are few high achievers, and large numbers stuck at the margins of literacy.

The detailed German research on PISA, conducted by the prestigious Max Planck Institute in Berlin, shows the connections between low achievement, social discrimination and the selective system. Children from manual worker backgrounds, and especially those with both parents born outside Germany, are most likely to attend the lowest level of school. Even when the researchers controlled for literacy, they found that children with similar attainment but from professional families were three times as likely to attend the top-tier Gymnasium or grammar school. Half the children with both parents born outside of Germany (and in most cases, the children had spent all their school years inside

Germany) attend the low-tier Hauptschule or secondary modern, compared with a quarter of the whole student population.

> 8.8% of German fifteen-year-olds reached the highest level, 5, in the literacy tests. The figures for New Zealand, Finland, Australia, Canada and Britain were between 15% and 20%.
>
> 10% of German pupils did not reach level 1, compared with an OECD average of 6%. In Korea, it was below 2%, in Finland and Canada about 3%, and below 5% in Britain. Only Brazil, Mexico, Latvia and Luxembourg scored lower than Germany.
>
> 23% of German pupils did not reach level 2, compared with 10% in Japan, Ireland and Canada and fewer still in Finland and Korea. (Baumert and Schümer 2002)

Selling our future

As well as increasing selection, the New Labour government have an agenda of privatisation for England. Every innovation seems tied to a significant handover of education to private financial interests – from education action zones to school buildings, individual schools to entire education authorities.

This is, of course, part of a global agenda across all public services. In Bolivia, popular protests were needed to stop the introduction of a law which would have forbidden people even to collect water on their own roofs rather than buying it from a private supplier. In 12,000 American schools, the pupils are forced to watch Channel One news and adverts every day (Klein 2000: 90). How long before British schools are persuaded to hand over their captive audience?

Richard Hatcher (2001: 63) lists some of the activities of the 'edubusiness' sector in Britain:

- school inspections (an industry worth over £100 million a year)
- the Private Finance Initiative (now re-branded Public Private Partnership) which hands over not just the construction but the running of school buildings)
- supply teachers
- professional development
- compulsory competitive tendering for school meals and maintenance
- local education authorities
- and finally, schools themselves.

The business world has been given a direct influence in the development of schooling, particularly in the inner cities, through the Education Action Zones, through direct ownership of city academies or by sponsoring specialist schools. Educational development is increasingly being defined as a source of profit rather than public benefit.

Often privatisation begins in the context of perceived failure and spreads from there. Education authorities in some of the poorest cities were inspected and subsequently privatised. The Public Private Partnership began by rebuilding decaying schools, but now an education minister is proposing to hand over every secondary school building in England into private ownership. How long before the landlord begins to determine what is taught under his roof?

There has been virtual silence from school improvement experts on this issue. Fortunately, other writers have been critical. They see the commodification of schooling as affecting the way its goals are being redefined, through a language of 'profitability, productivity, efficiency, value-addedness, and value-for-money or best-value' (Mahoney and Hextall 2000: 72).

> The balance has shifted from schools for the betterment of society through a more educated citizenry, to how best to control education by making it do its economic work through greater emphasis on vocationalism. (*ibid*: 32, quoting Smyth and Dow)

Characteristically, the very word *accountability* is a commercial metaphor.

Ironically, the consequent narrowing of focus can lead to forms of learning which do not match future commercial needs. According to the European Round Table of Industrialists (1994), employees are facing increasingly complex demands:

• in a theoretical sense, to understand complex relationships

• in a technical sense, to deal with program-controlled working tools

• in a social sense, to cooperate in teams

• in an organizational sense, to be able to cope with a spectrum of organizational, executive and evaluative tasks

• in an emotional sense, to identify with work and develop personal work-related motivation.

There appears to be a contradiction between capitalism's requirement for higher skills and its need for social control: on the one hand, it calls for qualities such as initiative and cooperation, but on the other, it would be subversive to go too far in that direction.

Forces of resistance

- Andy Hargreaves and Michael Fullan (1998) argue that teachers must connect up with the wider community in a discussion of worthwhile educational goals and methods.

- Some education systems have sustained a different sense of purpose. Until defeated in the wave of xenophobia after September 11 2001, progressive education ministers in Denmark pursued a democratic vision for education.

- There are strong voices of opposition and widespread attempts to develop alternatives in the United States. Extensive research refuting government policy appears in Phi Delta Kappan and the teachers' co-operative Rethinking Schools publishes powerful counter-arguments to privatisation, as well as reports of radical curriculum developments and different models of school.
  (www.pdkintl.org/kappan; www.rethinkingschools.org)

- Forces of resistance in Britain include teacher unions; subject associations such as NATE (National Association of Teachers of English); political organisations such as the Socialist Alliance in England and the Scottish Socialist Party; the Campaign for State Education and other alliances campaigning against the destruction of comprehensive education. There is a clear basis and need for a broad campaigning alliance.

The 'market' of school choice

The education market serves not only to redefine educational aims, but also to determine educational distribution. The Thatcher government emphasised parental choice, even to the extent of forcing some schools to admit more children than they had room for. This led to increased social and academic division between schools (Woods and Levacic 2002) as local pecking-orders developed, with the stigmatisation of teachers and pupils in unfavourably positioned schools. The attainment gap has risen in England and Wales.

School mix is an important factor. Whereas more advantaged children may do well in almost any environment, their absence from some schools can make a big difference to the education of others (see Thrupp 1999). Not only are better educated parents not involved in campaigning for improved resources, the cultural capital passed on in their families does not enter the common pool of intelligence.

In many cities, parental choice works in reverse: schools are choosing parents. Many nominally comprehensive schools interview parents as well as children – a system which may be more discriminatory than selection by exam. It has also led to racial segregation through white flight when parents drive their children to mainly white suburban or faith schools.

In the more competitive areas, children begin to feel they have failed if they can't get into the 'better' schools (Rudduck 2001: 21). There has been a huge increase in private tutoring in the attempt to secure higher test scores at the time of transfer, and middle-class mothers are investing enormous effort into securing advantage (Reay 2002). Children are quickly learning the dishonesty of self-marketing. A 12-year-old boy in a high-prestige London 'comprehensive' explained to me how he had passed the interview by claiming to read books or do homework when he arrived home from primary school; his friends who openly admitted going out to play football were rejected.

For other schools, the downward spiral is almost impossible to control, especially those which are surrounded by higher achieving schools, e.g. schools with sixth forms, church schools and specialist schools. If a less prestigious school has vacant places, it must subsequently admit pupils who are excluded by the surrounding schools. The exclusion process may be underhand, as unscrupulous heads suggest to parents that it would be wiser to take their troublesome adolescents elsewhere rather than risk being expelled.

Forces of resistance

• Tim Brighouse, as Director of Education in Birmingham, was able to sustain inter-school cooperation and minimise the tendency to compete. Innovative curriculum activities run by the University of the First Age and the Children's University brought together a mix of schools.

• Government plans are challenged whenever ministers speak to public audiences and trade union conferences. The impossible stress of defending the indefensible was conceivably a factor behind the sudden resignation of education minister Estelle Morris. It was noticeable that proposals to privatise all secondary school buildings and for low-paid classroom assistants to teach whole classes had to be announced by her junior colleagues.

• Privatisation is angering all public-service unions, and some union conferences have responded by withdrawing financial support from the Labour Party.

All this has a direct impact on educational achievement. The creation of an underclass of schools for an underclass of children is likely to create a trough of low achievement which no amount of pressure by the account-ability police will remedy.

'Dividing the sheep from the goats'

I have never understood this phrase, since goats are clearly more intelli-gent and independent than sheep. Maybe it is because the sheep are more marketable commodities and easier to herd. In present-day educational jargon, it is easier to 'add value' to a sheep.

Internally, schools are being driven to identify those animals which will fatten up best. The pressures of league tables, official accountability measures and high-stakes testing lead them to give special attention to pupils who are just below a key threshold (e.g. grade C or level 4).

Schools across Britain are facing increased pressure to stream and set. Although research in Britain and the USA is somewhat contradictory, and it is impossible to eliminate interference from a host of other variables, they have been fairly consistent in showing no overall rise in attainment through internal divisions. (For summaries, see for example Ireson and Hallam 2001 for Britain, or Gamoran's research in the USA and internationally.)

- Results in the upper sets may rise, but results in lower sets generally go down, and the attainment gap tends to grow

- Placement in a lower set – often influenced by social or behavioural factors as well as previous attainment – leads to lower self-esteem and to the growth of anti-school attitudes

- Schools tend to allocate more experienced or successful teachers to teach the higher sets

- Teachers' attitudes are affected by their understanding of a class's rank position, thus exacerbating polarisation. In the so-called Pygmalion studies, teachers were incorrectly told that some groups were more intelligent than others; this resulted in more challenging teaching and better results (Rosenthal and Jacobsen 1968)

- In primary schools, ability grouping within classes from an early age leads to a gender polarisation, concentrating boys in the lowest groups. This may result from developmental factors such as the physi-cal inability to produce neat handwriting. They develop an early self-image as low achievers. Recent research has shown that teachers choose to work directly with higher achieving groups of girls, whilst assigning classroom assistants to lower-attaining groups of boys (Kutnick 2002)

- Teachers' perceptions of 'ability' are often distorted by social prejudice (see Douglas and Barker-Lunn, as far back as 1964 and 1970). Early labelling and segregation soon becomes a self-fulfilling prophecy of low expectations for working-class and ethnic minority children.

There is international evidence that lower groups tend to have more restricted curricula, often including a tedious diet of decontextualised exercises. A major evaluation of *Title 1* (US federal funding for lower-achieving pupils) showed that pupils with lower reading scores were given only basic remedial work which did not help them 'develop the ability to analyze and communicate complex ideas' (National Assessment of Title 1 1998). Consequently, 'many students in Title 1 programs fall farther and farther behind as greater emphasis is placed on comprehension skills, problem-solving and reasoning' for other pupils as they get older. Instead of allowing them to catch up, this form of remediation leads into a cul-de-sac (see also BASRC 1999).

Internal divisions give strong messages to children about their personal value and 'ability'. They quickly internalise the implicit labelling, however well concealed. In official advice on school improvement, it is remarkable that the identification of high expectations as a factor in raising achievement is somehow kept separate from an appreciation of the cultural impact of internal segregation.

Some alternatives

The Accelerated School network, alongside intensive work on basic literacy skills, believes in high expectations for every student, and providing each student with powerful learning experiences that stress complex and engaging activities, relevant content and active discovery of curriculum objectives. Lessons are designed to be authentic, interactive, learner-centred, inclusive and connect between subjects. (see website)

With the right organisation and more challenging student-centred learning, higher achievers can excel in mixed groups. The Köln-Holweide comprehensive school in Germany emphasises co-operation and mutual help in mixed ability groups; it has achieved particularly good achievement for the brightest students. Co-ooperation is encouraged; if a student has a problem, he is expected first of all to seek help within his table group. (Sergiovanni 1994: 49–50)

In some circumstances, there may be tactical benefits from ability group-ing for particular purposes, though this needs to be carefully monitored alongside the impact on other classes. High achieving pupils sometimes need opportunities to work together as well as in mixed groups. Grove Primary School, Birmingham, has an accelerated mathematics class for older pupils; in this inclusive inner-city school where all children enjoy high respect and morale, a few children from each class come together for challenging mathematics activities, even gaining good GCSE grades at age 11 (five years early). The children clearly enjoy the experience, there is no hint of cramming but many opportunities to bounce ideas off one another and to set each other problems (Wrigley 2000: 82).

In Heywood Community School in Greater Manchester, only a handful of pupils ever gained good grades. Along with many other morale-boost-ing measures, a 'target group' was set up, with additional tutorial support from a popular teacher who accompanied the class from subject to subject. The tradition of low achievement was broken, and within four years, the proportion achieving five or more upper grades at GCSE had risen sixfold, to 47 per cent. This could not have happened, however, if a whole raft of other changes had not taken place to make all children in the school feel valued.

A key factor behind the insistence on more ability grouping is the pressure for whole-class teaching, despite growing understanding inter-nationally of methods of within-class differentiation. In its turn, this relates to the difficulties which arise from a pattern of secondary educa-tion in which subject specialists see each class for too short a time, and see too many children during the week to meet their various needs. A number of different models exist to create greater stability between pupils and a certain section of the teaching staff, with less emphasis on subject specialism.

Some alternatives

Falinge Park High School, Rochdale, allocates a class teacher to each class of 11-12 year olds for around 40% of their timetable to cover a range of sub-jects such as English, humanities and PSE and to serve as form tutor. Teachers work as a team to complement each others' specialist knowledge. The class teachers liaise with primary schools and other subject teachers, and respond to emotional and learning differences (Wrigley 2000: 90).

> The Coalition of Essential Schools (USA) divides schools into smaller units on the principle that no teacher can reasonably be expected to teach more than 80 different pupils in any year. Although British examples are scarce, the 'mini-school' or 'school within school' concept could provide a better means of raising standards for all pupils than the divisive path of current government policy.
> (See chapter 9 for further examples)

Education and poverty

There is a strong correlation between low achievement and poverty. This is a particularly serious problem in Britain, due to the high and chronic levels of child poverty.

Countries differ in the response they make to this. At its most extreme, in the USA, much less money is spent on schools in the poorest districts. School districts are often very small, so that more affluent suburbs don't have to subsidise the education of the poor in the inner city.

> A few American students are now attending 'public' schools that are funded at $15,000 or more per student per year, whereas other American students (who are stuck in poor communities within niggardly states) must make do with $3,000 or less per year in public school funding. (Biddle 1997)

A concern for school improvement has to include a willingness to campaign politically as well as to develop 'capacity' within schools.

Firstly, to campaign for much higher levels of spending for areas of deprivation. Funding is rigidly allocated according to formula in England, but education authorities in Scotland can choose to increase spending according to need. In England, the Excellence Fund has enabled some money to be targeted on inner cities, but is often focused on the relatively well off.

> The 'gifted and talented' programme provides mainly for those with proven talents in music and drama, i.e. those with prior experience and tuition outside school. HMI (2001b) point out the difficulty of identifying children with a potential. A more equitable programme would be based less on the notion of identifying a few individuals with talents, and more on providing opportunities for many children to develop new talents.

Secondly, there is the wider political fight against poverty. Children cannot focus on school when their families and neighbours are dogged by material anxieties. Some children clearly show greater resilience but this often depends on the right type of support. High and enduring unemployment levels have the most devastating impact on the morale of adolescents, who have fewer career role models and see little prospect of escape.

> The City of Glasgow now provides free fruit in schools to improve children's diet, and schools can use public funding to provide breakfasts. The Child Poverty Action Group, Scottish Socialist Party and other organisations recently joined forces to campaign for free and healthy school meals for all children – to improve levels of general health, to counter the high levels of poverty and overcome the stigma of the free meals queue. The resolution secured nearly a third of the votes in the Scottish Parliament, and will be tried again next year. During the campaign, it was discovered that two of the highest achieving countries, Finland and Sweden, already do this.

Finally, the strategies and cultures of relatively successful schools in poor areas need far greater study, and in particular the connections between the schools and the local situation. Such schools have often been able to develop new ways of relating to the experiences of their local communities. Often the first change is highly symbolic – raising the expectations of the entire community. Many deeper changes follow, but these imaginative first steps become symbols of determination that new opportunities can be created in the most troubled areas, as visible signals of new hope.

> **The first steps in turning a school are often imaginative and potent symbols of new hope:**
>
> • An ugly chimney dominating the entrance to Heywood Community Schools was painted with a mural of the statue of liberty
>
> • A conservatory was built onto the front of Blakeston Community School, Stockton-on-Tees, so that parents could meet staff in relaxed surroundings.

CHAPTER FIVE

Raising expectations – rethinking 'intelligence'

> *The intelligence of an individual is not a fixed quantity, a quantity that one cannot augment . . . We must protest and react against this brutal pessimism.*
>
> (Alfred Binet, 1913, inventor of the first 'intelligence test'
>
> *Our pupils are first generation academics.*
>
> (Jim Bleakley, headteacher)

In times of change, the capacity to deal with new situations and solve new problems can be more important than the acquisition of large amounts of knowledge. This capacity, which we variously call intelligence, ability or creativity, is central to the concept of educational improvement.

At the same time, a tacit belief that intelligence is fixed for life underlies so many of the actions of teachers and of the way schools are organised. It is too easy to speak blandly of 'high ability' and 'low ability' children, often based on limited evidence and a fair dose of cultural prejudice. Too many teachers still speak as if lower intelligence were a normal attribute of working-class children. Specific barriers to learning have often been confused with a general lack of intelligence: children placed in lower ability groups because their mother tongue is not English, and those in wheelchairs sent to special schools with a restricted curriculum.

The relevance of concepts of intelligence to the raising of expectations is demonstrated by Carol Dweck's research into the different responses of people who believe their intelligence is fixed from those who believe that it develops. The former tend to become defeatist when they fail at a task, believing that it has exposed their innate stupidity. They reject opportunities to learn by avoiding taking risks, for fear of what the out-come might reveal about their intelligence, whereas people who hold a developmental theory accept challenges more readily. People who believe

75

in fixed intelligence often believe that truly intelligent people don't need to make a great effort (Dweck 2002).

Many common beliefs about intelligence are rooted in an early 20th century psychology which was strongly influenced by the conditions and prejudices of the age. Recent research has made available more dynamic and hopeful models of intelligence which school improvement needs to debate and deploy.

The purpose of this chapter is

- to engage in what Foucault called 'archaeology of knowledge', by looking at the circumstances in which contemporary beliefs about ability developed – including a significant variation on the theme, the concept of language deficit

- to explore recent theories such as multiple and distributed intelligence

- to identify the significance of different assumptions and theories for school improvement.

Class, racism and IQ: a short history

Before the twentieth century, little emphasis was placed on the concept of intelligence as we now use the term. When Victorian writers used the term intellectual ability, for example, they seem to have had a more contextual view, referring to an ability to pursue particular activities within an assumed cultural environment. The relationship of ability to class was both explicit and direct; for most Victorian policy makers, it was simply unthinkable and intolerable to educate working-class children 'above their station in life'.

Different views of ability are generated in particular historical circumstances. There were cultural variants in Britain; within a Calvinist tradition of universal literacy, many teachers in rural Scotland assumed that poor spelling must be the result of a moral failing – idleness – to be cured by a good beating. In Pacific Rim countries, the prevalent notion appears to be that all children can learn the same things provided they work long enough at it – a theory which is not without benefits.

Changes occurred in early 20th century Britain for a combination of cultural and political reasons:

(a) Culturally, the eugenics movement was strong, and with it a common concern, shared even by progressive thinkers such as Wells, Shaw and the Webbs, that the quality of the British 'race' could decline if the poor (or worse still, the 'feeble minded') were allowed to breed so much. This had its roots in the transfer of Darwinist evolutionary theory to the human arena, within a hierarchical and imperialist society, and was to have murderous effects when it transferred to German fascist ideology. Since few tools were available to measure intelligence, phrenologists in the late Victorian period measured the size and shape of the skull to estimate its physical capacity to hold knowledge, while others simply assumed that upper-class people were born with more intelligence (See Chitty 2001 and Carey 1992).

(b) Politically, this period saw the rise of the Labour Movement, including a massive increase in trade union membership and the foundation of the Labour Party. Internationally, organised labour proved strong enough to stop war by revolution in Russia, Germany and elsewhere, and even in Britain the government was threatened by the anti-war and industrial revolt spreading from 'Red Clydeside'. It became too risky for governments to speak in patronising Victorian terms of educating boys and girls 'for their station in life' or of the general intellectual inferiority of the 'lower orders'. When employers' representatives were asked by the Consultative Committee on Higher Elementary Schools (1906) 'What is the kind of product most to be desired?', they answered bluntly 'To make them efficient members of the class to which they belong'. This is probably the last time, in a public document on education, that such crude class language appears.

> Faced with such increasing radical activity, the language of class arrogance was hardly appropriate. It was becoming no longer possible to dismiss the vast majority of working class children as being unfit to receive a secondary education because of their class alone. (Cowburn 1986: 122–125)

This, and the skills shortage after World War I, formed the context for the introduction of new ideas and practices. Though less overtly discriminatory, they continued to confine most working-class children to a cheap elementary education until they left school at 14, though a few proceeded into white-collar employment. (The different Scottish tradition already provided a well-marked route, with financial support, for some working-class boys and girls to go through university.)

The answer came in the form of intelligence testing. Alfred Binet, director of the psychology laboratory at the Sorbonne, had previously developed a battery of test items, on the request of the minister of public education, to identify children who needed additional help to benefit from a normal education. The items were a mixture of logical and practical tasks from which a score was derived as a general indication of acquired abilities. From diverse and rather arbitrary tasks such as distinguishing ugly from pretty faces, naming the months of the year in correct order and finding three rhymes for a word within a minute, a score was calculated; the age at which that score was typically attained was noted; and, by subtraction, the difference between mental age and physical age. It is important to note that Binet saw his test score as a general indicator of acquired abilities at a particular point in time. He totally rejected the idea of a fixed innate intelligence.

> What most amazes me about Alfred Binet . . . was the conclusion he did not jump to, the theory he did not assert . . . He figured out a way to measure intelligence. However, he held back from the obvious conclusion – intelligence as a pure essence measured out more to some people and less to others. He left the door open for learnable intelligence. He focused simply on how one could put a number to a phenomenon – the phenomenon of intelligent behaviour. (David Perkins 1995: 23–4)

The adoption of his methods in Britain and America gave a radically different twist: intelligence testing was thought to identify innate intelligence and related to social class (Britain) and racial difference (USA). In place of substraction, a new method was adopted of dividing mental age by chronological age to give an intelligence quotient (IQ) which would supposedly remain the same through life. Binet's fluid notion of intelligence was grafted on to the phrenologists' mechanistic concept of brain *capacity*:

> Capacity must obviously limit content. It is impossible for a pint jug to hold more than a pint of milk. (C Burt, 1937)

In Britain Cyril Burt and others immediately linked intelligence testing to their firm prejudice that working-class children were genetically poorly equipped (see Cowburn 1986; Rose, Kamin and Lewontin 1984).

Burt's arguments lacked logic, but were well rooted in class prejudice and fitted the contemporary intellectual climate. While still an undergraduate student at Oxford, he had noted:

> The problem of the very poor – chronic poverty: little prospect of the solution of the problem without the forcible detention of the wreckage of society or otherwise preventing them from propagating their own species. (in Rose *et al* 1984: 87)

Significantly, Burt was launched on his career with the Greater London Council as the first educational psychologist in the English speaking world on the recommendation of his father's friend Sir Francis Galton, who first coined the word *eugenics*. Burt built his reputation on a series of studies of identical twins brought up by different families; the high correlation between the separated twins' intelligence levels was said to prove that intelligence must be hereditary. Only after his death was it discovered that the research was fictitious: the tests were never identified, the research assistants had emigrated years before they supposedly administered the tests, the adoptive parents' intelligence quotients were simply guesses, and the data was nowhere to be found (*ibid*: 98, which also critiques other identical-twin studies).

Burt's research reports would have been discredited during his lifetime if his arguments had not been ideologically convenient. IQ tests were used in the USA and Britain to shunt vast numbers of working-class and minority children into inferior and dead-end educational paths (*ibid*: 87), not to mention providing justification for the sterilisation of 'morons' and the preference given to immigrants who came to the USA from North-West Europe.

In America the emphasis was on racial difference. Tests which asked Polish, Italian and Jewish applicants for entry permits to give the nicknames of professional baseball teams, or to say whether a 'Caucasian' or a 'Negroid' face was prettier, were used to reject potential immigrants on the grounds of their supposed low intelligence. Psychologists such as Terman, Spearman and Goddard presented the American authorities with seemingly scientific evidence of the superiority of white 'Anglo-Saxons'. There was no satisfactory explanation of what was being tested – Boring (1923) defined intelligence tautologically as 'what intelligence tests measure' – but the practice took hold.

> Stated in its boldest form, our thesis is that the chief determiner of human conduct is a unitary mental process which we call intelligence; that this process is conditioned by a nervous mechanism which is inborn; that the degree of efficiency to be attained by that nervous mechanism and the consequent grade of intellectual or mental level for each individual is determined by the kind of chromosomes that come together with the union of the germ cells; that it is but little affected by any later influences except such serious accidents as may destroy part of the mechanism. (Goddard 1920, cited by Perkins 1995)

The concept was used ideologically to support politically conservative arguments. In a lecture at Princeton University in 1919, Goddard was already using the 'fixed character of mental levels' as the reason why some were rich and others poor, some employed and others unemployed:

How can there be such a thing as social equality with this wide range of mental capacity? . . . As for an equal distribution of the wealth of the world, that is equally absurd. (Rose *et al* 1984: 86)

The concept of fixed intelligence survived despite overwhelming evidence that test scores rose substantially as a result of education. IQ tests are periodically restandardised against a mean of 100 for the current population; strange effects emerge when they are re-standardised against a constant level of difficulty.

- A massive rise was recorded in the average IQ of Italian Americans over a generation, as formal education was extended (see Perkins 1995: 40–64)

- The average IQ of American services recruits in World War II was a standard deviation higher than in World War I (Humphreys 1989)

- Conversely, the measured IQ of African Americans was found to decline substantially as they went through school

- The correlation between tests administered a decade apart was shown to be less than .70 (Humphreys 1989)

- The Dutch military tests all young men, using Raven's Progressive Matrices (a non-verbal mental ability test). In 1952 31% scored more than 24 out of 40; by 1981 this had risen to 82%

- When average IQ scores for a British sample were adjusted to maintain constant levels of difficulty, the average had risen from 73 in 1942 to 100 in 1992 (Flynn 1999)

The challenge to the hegemonic concept of IQ was assisted through the struggle for comprehensive schools, when it was noticed that some children who had failed the 11+ examination went on to succeed in examinations at age 16.

One secondary modern school for girls serving a working-class district in a large industrial city, which took in only children who had *failed* to get into either a grammar or a selective central school, entered girls for the O level examination in 1954. Of those who gained five or more passes, one had had an IQ of 97 on entry to the school in 1949, another an IQ of 85. This was at a time when an IQ of 115 or over was generally considering to be necessary to profit from examination courses. And other schools were soon in a position to tell similar success stories, so that there were real problems involved in defending the psychometrists' standpoint. (Simon 1955: 64–66)

Nowadays the scientific basis for theories of innate general intelligence has little support, despite some recent attempts to justify ideas of racial superiority. However, at the level of popular – and professional – folk mythology, it is alive and kicking. Its impact on academic expectations and achievement would be an interesting subject for School Improvement research, since it is difficult for teachers to raise their expectations of pupils while the ideology of fixed ability levels remains strong. School improvement requires a rigorous debate of such debilitating myths.

Language deficit

Wilf Cowburn (1986) continues his political history of constructs of ability and working-class achievement by examining the concept of *language deficit* developed by Basil Bernstein. Once again, a convenient argument was adopted into professional and popular thinking on the basis of fundamentally flawed research.

After Burt's theories were exposed, and despite the establishment of comprehensive schools, working-class achievement remained relatively low and a new theory had to be developed. Bernstein corrrectly identified a disjunction between the cultures of home and school, and a difference in patterns of language use. Sadly, though critical of the decontextualised learning normal within schools, he chose to focus on the working-class family as the source of the problem.

The notion of language deficit had already been applied to Caribbean creoles; it was falsely argued that their grammatical deviation from Standard English prevented logical thinking. Bernstein argued that working-class families use a 'restricted code' which is generally sufficient, in a familiar environment, for talking about things you can feel and see, but which is seriously prejudicial to intellectual development. He acknowledged that 'middle-class families' (i.e. non-manual occupations) also use a restricted code when the meaning is clear:

A: Tea, dear?
B: Ah hum.

but argued that these families also have at their disposal an elaborated code, allowing for explicit reference to events which are not physically present.

Labov (1969) in New York and Rosen (1972) in London challenged this deficit theory, exposing its crude and misleading generalisations. They gave illustrations of the discourses through which complex political and philosophical issues are debated in marginalised communities. Labov

makes the point that children had been taken from the Harlem ghetto
into an alien environment and then judged by the deficit researchers to be
inarticulate. Teachers can easily make the same mistake, confusing a
child's anxieties in school or difference in linguistic expectations with an
inability to communicate. Labov met with African American adolescents
in their own neighbourhoods, and found them extremely articulate about
a range of high-level philosophical, theological and political issues,
though using a different linguistic code and register.

Bernstein's theory spread like wildfire. His generalisation that working-
class mothers smack their children rather than explain to them became
urban myth among teachers. There was no quantitative evidence for
generalising his anecdote of the stereotypical middle-class mother who
says 'Please sit down, dear, you might hurt yourself if the bus stops
suddenly' while the working-class mum responds to 'Why?' with a slap.
The formal research which took place on different speech patterns was
logically flawed. Children were presented with cartoon drawings of boys
playing football. One boy kicks a ball over a fence, breaking a window; the
boys run off, leaving the neighbour shouting angrily. The working-class
boys, we are told, tended to use pronouns (a marker of restricted code):
'He kicks the ball through the window, then they run away' whereas the
middle-class boys used nouns (elaborated code). Since the children had
the cartoon in front of them all the time they were speaking, pronouns
were perfectly sensible. The middle-class children simply had a better
appreciation of the groundrules – the expectations of a different register
for formal quasi-educational settings.

Despite these problems, the concept of language deficit prospered
throughout the 1970s and into the 1980s and served to justify lower
expectations of inner-city students. It is still important for School
Improvement to learn from sociolinguists such as Rosen and Labov, to
prevent confusion between linguistic deficit and different social registers.
This is not to say that working-class children must not be helped towards
the 'elaborated code' of more abstract language, but simply that the
process involves building upon and working through, rather than reject-
ing, more contextualised uses of language.

The concept of language deficit, as originally applied to Caribbean
creoles and Black American English, was fundamentally prejudiced. It
was wrongly argued that double negatives or the frequent omission of the
verb 'to be' indicated illogicality. In fact, double negatives are the norm in
French, and neither Russian nor Arabic uses 'to be' in the present tense.
The argument of linguistic inadequacy indicates social prejudice, not
linguistic science. The confusion went far beyond these specifics, and

was mixed with older prejudice about the supposed inferiority of regional dialects and languages.

> Draw a sharp distinction between the language of the home and the street and the language the school is trying to achieve. Teachers should not set children to talk or write about their homes or neighbourhoods, because that would be inviting them to use the wrong language.
> (*The Teaching of English in the Elementary Schools of London*, 1929; cited in Pradl 1982)

In their different ways, both these 20th century models, innate intelligence and language deficit, provided discursive protection for practices which systematically failed working-class pupils. A number of pedagogical and cultural issues emerge from this which should be of keen interest to the School Improvement project:

- questions about the social and experiential development of intelligence
- the relationship between practical activity and theoretical learning
- the forms of language which are valued in schools
- the accumulation of facts and concepts in a low-experience environment
- the way in which working-class children experience figures of authority
- the ways in which children of different backgrounds internalise their positioning as passive and relatively silent learners at school
- the relationship between school learning and community needs as experienced by working-class children and adolescents.

Positive strategies similar to those developed to assist bilingual pupils' transition from everyday transactional and conversational English into an academic code should be explored in order to enhance working-class achievement. This would involve structured opportunities to articulate problems, form hypotheses and suggest solutions, in which the teacher's interventions scaffold the learner's shift towards a more academic register by paraphrasing students' ideas and making available more formal explanations in alternative linguistic codes.

Cultural capital

Currently, we appear to be in a state of flux. There is at present no dominant or explicit concept of ability as we float between notions of hard work, genetic capacity, and socialisation. The accountability culture may be leading us back to a simpler moral emphasis on the value of persistent effort. A by-product of this is that many children may internalise their lack of success as a sense of personal inadequacy.

Throughout all these shifts, the common-sense notion of intelligence or ability is resolutely individualised: it sounds odd to speak about a collective intelligence, i.e. the acquired ability of a group of people to solve a problem. (See page 86 below)

We urgently need to retheorise ability in the context of a divided society and for the age in which we live. Bourdieu's theory of *cultural capital* provides an important clue. He argues that the principal cause of educational disadvantage is not linguistic weakness but a clash of cultures. The children of professional parents with a university education unconsciously pass on to their children extensive cultural knowledge and habits which are positively received in school (Bourdieu and Paseron 1970). The different cultural knowledge of children from marginalised communities, on the other hand, does not function as capital because its value goes unrecognised by teachers and there is a mismatch with the discourse of schools.

This moves the argument from an individualistic understanding of intelligence towards a socio-cultural one. The ability of more privileged children to succeed in formal educational settings is not a greater intelligence inherited from parents, but a social habitus which derives from a cultural environment. In considering ways of making valued cultural capital available to working-class and ethnic minority children, we need to avoid simplistic solutions such as teaching a collection of cultural facts, or the danger of conveying a sense that working class children's cultural frameworks are inferior.

Multiple intelligences

Howard Gardner characterises school learning as predominantly *decontextualized* and *notational*.

> We now place a great premium on amassing 20–50 students together in a classroom for 6–8 hours a day over many years, disallowing most kinds of physical activity or contact, discouraging socializing, and saving rewards for those who can pore over books or papers, make small squiggles on lined pieces of paper, repeat back what has been told to them, and on occasional 'high-stake' tests, provide precise forms of information on demand. (Gardner *et al* 1996: 252)

Such practices lead to circular thinking about intelligence.

> Our definitions . . . of intelligence have been based in significant measure on what individuals are expected to do in school. If, for example, school is the site par excellence for notational work in a decontextualized setting, and if tests of intelligence require the manipulation of symbols in a decontextualized setting, then it is scarcely surprising when individuals who score well on an intelligence test do well in school, or vice versa. (*ibid*: 254)

Gardner proposes a different model – *multiple intelligences*, as opposed to a single general intelligence. He derives his model of distinct abilities from evidence such as child prodigies and studies of brain-damage, as well as uneven development in education and everyday life. For example, we may find little correlation between bodily-kinaesthetic intelligence in footballers and the skills they require in school – or, as we often see, for television interviews. Gardner's first model has seven intelligences, though he has since suggested revising the number:

- linguistic
- musical
- logical-mathematical
- spatial
- bodily-kinaesthetic
- intrapersonal
- interpersonal.

Gardner has warned against his theory leading to new forms of discrimination, such as the idea that black teenagers have an hereditary ability at sport but not at maths. He opposes the suggestion that schools should simply concentrate on areas of strength. While insisting that intelligences represent potential for learning or problem solving, rather than an acquired skill, he recognises that they can only materialise in particular cultural situations: thus, Mozart and Robbie Williams both have musical intelligence but could not compose each other's songs. (Perhaps the difficulties around this point should lead us to move further away from the genetic explanations which seem to persist in Gardner's theory and towards a more environmental model of *acquired* multiple intelligences.)

The concept of multiple intelligences is liberating in a number of ways. It makes it more difficult to place children in rank order. It prevents us devaluing those children who are less successful in decontextualised notational learning. It has also stimulated practical experimentation in using a wider sensory range to teach difficult ideas.

Multiple intelligence theory in practice

- A class of nine-year-olds miming different adverbs in a game of charades, as a step towards consolidating the concept of parts of speech: 'She said it . . . joyfully/cautiously/boldly'

- A weekend workshop on *Macbeth* where each scene is developed according to one of the multiple intelligences: musical, intrapersonal, spatial

- A school in Copenhagen built on a design which provides particular spaces where the different intelligences can be developed.

We also need to be wary of the dangers. In England, the government are rapidly increasing the number of specialist schools which will select a proportion of pupils at age 11 on the basis of ability in specific fields, from mathematics to languages, from sport to business. This may seem to be an advance on the idea of a fixed general intelligence, but since there are no credible mechanisms for identifying potential in these fields, the system can only prove to be a new form of social discrimination. It will serve to select those children whose backgrounds have given them greater opportunities to experience these fields, or whose parents can argue most articulately for their admission.

Distributed intelligence

We normally think of 'intelligence' in resolutely individualistic terms – the idea of a 'collective intelligence' sounds like science fiction – yet there are many instances when it becomes apparent that this is not the only way of thinking about potential and ability.

- Wandering round a Renaissance art gallery, it is striking how much Italian 15th Century paintings have in common: apart from a few remnants of an earlier Gothic style or the odd El Greco, it takes truly expert knowledge to distinguish between individual artists without the labels

- Writing or playing music within a particular genre or period means partaking of the shared intelligence of those who have gone before

- Bourdieu's 'cultural capital' might be seen as the collective intelligence of a privileged social class

- Similarly, groups of adolescents with their own sub-culture(s) share knowledge and patterns of behaviour, and their ways of working and habits of interaction represent a capacity for solving particular types of problem and skilfully undertaking certain forms of action

- When we watch a group of mechanics standing round a car engine trying to diagnose a difficult fault by listening, experimenting, adjusting, we see a shared activity whose success depends on combined intelligence.

In all these examples, the sum is greater than the parts. It is remarkable, then, that so much emphasis is placed in schools on children working in isolation; even when children sit around a table and are said to be working in groups, close observation generally reveals them to be working on separate tasks while occasionally helping one another.

A Harvard-based research team including David Perkins, Gavriel Salomon, Roy Pea, Howard Gardner and others, has been working since the late 1980s on alternative concepts of intelligence. (The Project Zero website shows numerous projects for raising achievement in schools.)

One key idea is the concept of *distributed intelligence*. Perkins (1995: 322) suggests that intelligence can be distributed in three ways:

- *Physical*: We rely on physical artifacts as simple as note pads and as complex as computer-aided design systems and beyond to do various kinds of remembering and computing for us

- *Social*: We do not typically think solo but in teams where different people bring different abilities to the mix, and collaboration moves the general enterprise along

- *Symbolic*: We do not think in bare thoughts but thoughts clothed in symbol systems, including natural languages with their rich vocabulary of thinking-oriented terms and a variety of notional and graphic symbol systems.

This exploration of intelligence builds upon Engels' understanding that individual skills depend upon socially-developed tools, and Vygotsky's subsequent conception of language as the social tool which enables individual cognition (see also Cole and Engeström 1993).

A few familiar examples might illustrate this way of thinking:

- To prevent overload, we sometimes use reminders (alarms, lists, post-it notes, other people) to help us sequence an activity

- Writing frames can provide children with a structural map and a reminder of some typical starter phrases so that they can concentrate on expressing their personal content
- As I am writing this book, and struggling to concentrate on an impossibly wide range of ideas and sources, the task is eased by my computer's error checker, a list of chapter headings, an earlier text written for other purposes which I can copy and paste, and, on the floor around me, a circle of key books needed to reference the present chapter
- In mathematics we draw graphical models or use graphic calculators to provide a visual reference, and often to mediate between verbal ideas and physical experiences
- Architects working in different locations might share their ideas for a new building electronically, using the software to sketch arches or display from different angles (from Perkins 1995).

> Roy Pea (1993:70) provides a metaphor for distributed intelligence by inventing a special tape-measure for foresters. This device would incorporate a conversion formula and a value for π, such that the forester can measure a tree of 2.5m circumference and read off 0.4m (the radius) from the tape measure.

The distribution of intelligence is not a replacement for the individual, but recognises that, in real life, our ability to solve problems and deal with new situations often derives from the 'person-plus' not the 'person-solo' (Perkins 1993: 88). Schools, however, often regard this as suspect, preferring situations in which an individual works with nothing but a pen, and even this is mainly used to record answers rather than to sketch strategies and solutions. We have seen much of this tendency recently in the emphasis on mental calculations and the suspicion of calculators – an attitude which would have eliminated slide-rules and logarithm books for my generation!

Clarity about this issue is important for school improvement. When some children repeatedly fail with detailed calculations, we need to consider the wisdom of compelling them to do more and more, against the possibility of distributing part of the thinking to a calculator so that the learner can engage in more interesting ventures.

> Children whose different talents are developing at different speeds need experiences which will boost their confidence and give them a taste of success – rather than seeing themselves labelled as comparative failures in the 3 Rs. (Tim Brighouse, 2002)

Individuals obviously need to move between situations, and take with them knowledge, skills and the memory of previous solutions. One way of looking at this is as a residue of those other occasions when we have worked with tools, colleagues and sets of notes. We obviously cannot rely totally on the right cultural tools being available, and schools need to plan for capacity to adapt to new situations and transfer understanding and strategies. Perkins reminds us, however, that working with other people and with tools isn't an avoidance of personal learning: it is often the best route to it. By distributing lower-level aspects of a task, we can focus on the higher-level ones. He uses the example of the Geometric Supposer, a computer program 'designed to restore exploration and discovery to the teaching of Euclidean geometry'. (For further examples, see Gavriel Salomon, ed, 1993, *Distributed Cognitions*, and David Perkins 1992, *Smart Schools*, two books which are rich with theory and practical ideas for schools.)

The Geometric Supposer provides a 'constructive arena'

- It makes geometric construction easy: a user can request that a triangle be drawn, an altitude dropped, and so on.

- It makes measuring such constructions to check conjectures very easy: for example a student can request a measurement of two sides of a triangle to see if they are equal.

- It makes retesting a conjecture on different versions of the same process extremely easy: the student can repeat the operation with a new randomly-sized triangle to explore an hypothesis. (Perkins 1993: 102)

Rethinking intelligence – rethinking learning

This is an exciting period in terms of new social models of learning. School improvement needs to share in the theory as well as disseminating the practice.

This chapter has only skimmed the surface of a growing list: the implications of emotional intelligence (Goleman), the many variants of thinking skills, children's philosophy (Lipman and others) and so on. Perkins uses the concept 'metacurriculum' (1992: 99–130), proposing that students simultaneously learn ways of thinking and areas of content. His analysis of forms of learning which fail to raise achievement is illuminating: fragile knowledge, inert knowledge, naïve knowledge and ritual knowledge (*ibid*: 20–27). His argument that intelligence is *learnable* is the best antidote to the pessimistic concept of innate intelligence: it raises more hopeful possibilities of raising achievement than the constant pressure for intensification.

We need more than a bag of tricks: we need different theoretical models with the potential to generate new learning activities. We also need to think of the complexity of young people's learning in the world today, wonderfully illustrated in Nick Hornby's novel *About a Boy*, with its complex illustrations of social and cultural learning and emotional intelligence.

Bentley argues that our information age requires forms of ability or *creativity*, involving:

- the ability to formulate new problems, rather than depending on others to define them

- the ability to transfer what one learns across different contexts

- the ability to recognise that learning is incremental and involves making mistakes

- the capacity to focus one's attention in pursuit of a goal

- secure trusting relationships and environments in which people are prepared to take risks and learn from failure

- freedom of action, so that people can make real choices over what they do and how they try to do it

- variations of context, so that learners can transfer and make connections

- the right balance between skills acquisition and challenging new activities

- interactive exchange of knowledge and ideas

- real world outcomes, so that creativity and motivation are reinforced by the experience of making an impact and giving benefit to others. (Bentley 2001: 136–137)

He suggests that the 'scope for continuous improvement in output and productivity within the present infrastructure' is limited. Some serious rethinking is required, as schools are increasingly at odds with the more challenging environments which learners will later encounter. Schools need to be restructured as learning communities, as stimulating and cooperative environments on a human scale, which can connect with the wider problem-rich communities in which innovation flourishes.

CHAPTER SIX

Curriculum, class and culture

Questions From A Worker Who Reads
... The young Alexander conquered India.
Did he go alone?
Caesar beat the Gauls.
Didn't he even have a cook with him?
Philip of Spain wept when his armada sank.
Was he the only one to cry?

(Bertolt Brecht)

The literature on school improvement, for all its talk of vision, mission and values, is strangely silent about curriculum. It tacitly accepts the legitimacy and benefit of a curriculum imposed from above. The collegiality it invites does not, apparently, extend to jointly discussing what should be taught and why. In the English context in particular, it is as if school culture and the capacity for change are unimpeded by an imposed National Curriculum which was designed with barely a thought for learner motivation.

There are some major problems with an imposed curriculum.

(i) The imposition of a curriculum assumes a linear view of reality. The curriculum is seen as the starting point: first the curriculum, then work out how to 'deliver' it, and finally measure how much has been learnt. This model, formalised by Tyler (1949), appeals to common sense and bureaucratic minds, but is really far too simple.

The Curriculum is never finally defined on paper. The way we teach can radically affect the curriculum as experienced by our students. The way it is tested washes back on both.

(ii) It quickly acquires a false sense of permanence. People begin to assume that the curriculum has always looked like this. The National Curriculum (England and Wales) was a complete upstart, a strange

91

> Curriculum is reshaped, remade, reborn, recoded in what we do with kids in classrooms. Pedagogy re-mediates, frames and rearticulates what will count as knowledge in classrooms. So no matter how we theorise or 'fix' the curriculum – either centrally or locally – it won't make much difference if our pedagogy isn't up to scratch.
>
> Basil Bernstein has long held that assessment and evaluation will ultimately pull curriculum and pedagogy along. Thirty years of research on teacher behaviour tells us that as soon as we bring in 'high stakes' assessment . . . teachers will suss out what is being assessed and torque or reorient the curriculum and pedagogy back towards the 'high stakes'. (Allan Luke, 1999)

mixture of advanced thinking, political arrogance and ideological censorship, but within three or four years it began to look natural, just part of the way schools do things.

(iii) We forget that a curriculum is but a selection from that vast array of knowledge, skills and emotions that may be worth passing down to the next generation. It assumes that those who designed it know what our students will need. It assumes that those who have selected this curriculum have made a neutral decision, and have our best interests at heart.

(iv) It creates a false sense of insecurity: teachers and pupils become so concerned with covering the syllabus that they fail to construct from it *their* curriculum, their set of meanings, their understanding of the world which may act as a guide in a future yet unknown.

Improvement has to be rooted in the identification of educational aims. Improvement is a moral category, not just a technical pursuit. If improvement simply involved delivering whatever curriculum is imposed, then an efficiently taught racist or fundamentalist curriculum would do just as well.

'Curriculum is a selection from the culture'

Raymond Williams' concept of a *selective tradition* (1961) is crucial to a critical understanding of curriculum. Williams was personally engaged in transforming the teaching of English literature and culture at Cambridge into a subject that was able to stir some of the brightest students of the generation. Having grown up in a railway worker's family on the Welsh border, he struggled to understand the fixed canon of an hereditary elite culture. He successfully linked the study of literary texts to their political environment, shedding new light on Dickens and Gaskell and Hardy, reconnecting novels to contemporary political texts and the wider culture, and denying the assumption that what we call Literature is radically separate and on a higher plane than politics.

Williams sought to understand the processes of selection, and the forces that shape it, in order to disrupt the fixity of that particular canon of texts known as English Literature. This raises the issue of social power and the impact of a class structure on culture. We should question the influence, albeit complex and refracted, of an elite's

> vision of legitimate knowledge, one that in the process of enfranchising one group's cultural capital disenfranchises another's. (Apple 1993: 49)

The concept of selection is crucial. With his formulation 'Curriculum is a selection from the culture', Denis Lawton (1978) attempted to transfer Williams' insight to the school situation. This was liberating to a point, since curriculum no longer appeared normal or natural, but Lawton risked losing Williams' critical edge. His statement begs some questions:

(i) the definite article suggests a singular entity, whether an authoritative canon or a broadly accepted common culture

(ii) it is important to ask why particular items are selected, who has done the selecting, for whom and to what ends.

Since then, many attempts have been made to analyse the selected curriculum in terms of social and ideological direction. My preferred model comes from Stephen Kemmis and colleagues (Victoria, Australia). The state government had commissioned a team to consider a vocational alternative to the traditional academic curriculum, but their response was broader and more critical:

> Educational principles are social principles. Our views of education, and hence of schooling, have their justification in views of society and the proper role of education for participation in the life and work of society.

> The problem is that people tend to construe differences between codes in education as differences of style. And that hides the fact that there are profound disagreements about what education is and what it is for. (Kemmis, Cole and Suggett 1983: 8)

They developed a model based on three *orientations*, which I have attempted to model below (page 94).

(i) **Neo-classical/vocational**. A *neo-classical* (academic) curriculum and a *vocational* curriculum share the same orientation. Both fit people into society as it stands, but for different roles: manual workers require clearly defined competences, whereas managerial and professional roles

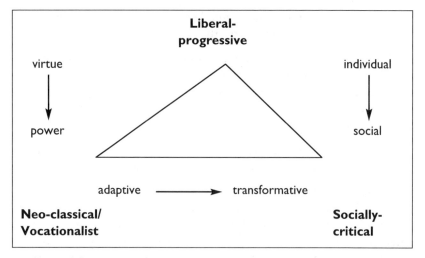

require higher levels of general education and abstract universalised thinking.

Both are construed in terms of being realistic, with a belief that 'education merely reflects the principles of the wider society'. The world is 'hierarchically ordered . . . and the best endowed will find their way to rewarding positions'. A certainty is assumed about what is worth knowing, based on 'time-honoured beliefs' but 'reinterpreted for the modern world'. (*ibid*)

(ii) **Liberal-progressive** This descriptor identifies some limiting features of progressivism, as found for example in progressive primary schools or versions of secondary English. It tends to be individualistic, disregarding social pressures and structures.

> Liberal humanism is a suburban moral ideology, limited in practice to largely interpersonal matters. It is stronger on adultery than on armaments, and its valuable concern with freedom, democracy and individual rights are simply not concrete enough. (Terry Eagleton 1983: 107)

It is less authoritarian and more open than a neo-classical or vocational curriculum, and creates valuable spaces for learning, but is not as radical as its advocates claim. It rejects the subordination of education to employers' requirements – though sometimes overstating the case, as if pupils wouldn't ever need to earn a living. Its preferred way to improve society is by promoting personal growth: developing 'a sense of the good, true and beautiful in every child'. Its weakness is that it is 'individualistic, moralistic, and apolitical'.

(iii) **Socially-critical** The team then identify, and clearly favour, this third orientation. 'If changes are to be wrought in our social structure, then individual virtue and individual action will be insufficient to bring them about. They must be brought about by collective action capable of confronting unjust and irrational social structure.' We need to reach a 'critical and historical understanding of current culture', and to engage in a 'collective search for solutions'. Though sharing with vocationalists the demand for relevance and contextualised learning, this orientation is different; socially-critical educators try to weaken the boundaries between school and community in order to engage learners in community-based action and analysis, rather than simply to give them skills.

*   *   *

An understanding of curricular orientations is needed in order to evaluate the direction of educational change. Without it, we are unable to distinguish better from merely different, faster or worse. Improvement means different things to different people – a dilemma which we cannot escape simply by concentrating on culture, capacity or change management. What would count as improvement in a fascist dictatorship? in a Cistercian monastery? for a clan of new age travellers? An improvement for the rich man in his castle can make life harder for the poor man at the gate.

There can be no authentic discussion about improvement without a discussion about values and social position. The failure to engage in such a discussion simply confirms the status quo, or rather, the direction of change imposed by the most powerful.

For example, when evaluating the Literacy Hour in English primary schools, we need to look beyond test results to examine which literary practices are emphasised and what messages children receive? Is the academic/vocationalist goal of functional literacy being pursued at the expence of empathy and expression (the liberal-progressive emphasis) or critical literacy?

Education for Citizenship sounds quite a radical innovation, but might easily decline into a conservative Civics, involving factual knowledge about constitutional structures combined with a dose of patriotic duty. A liberal-progressive version might involve compassion for those less fortunate and some 'active citizenship' in the form of charitable acts. A socially-critical version requires a bolder selection of controversial issues, and a pedagogy combining knowledge, empathy and collective emancipatory action.

Curriculum, race and social class

Although it is common to challenge the imposed curriculum in terms of a multicultural or antiracist alternative, it has become almost impossible to debate a curriculum for pupils who are marginalised by their position in the class structure. The term Community Curriculum is rather too vague. Vocational alternatives prescribed for disaffected pupils increase motivation, but young people surely need something more than skills for employment.

Clarity on this matter is particularly important at the present time. The Thatcherite curriculum of 1988, despite the general neo-liberal politics of her government, was significantly neo-conservative in its insistence on a rigid curriculum for all children based on an authorised and traditional body of knowledge. (See Apple 1996 for the relationship between neo-conservativism and neo-liberalism.) New Labour has, in some respects, brought curriculum policy more into line with neo-liberal tendencies. The concept of a broad and balanced curriculum, albeit distorted by a conservative vision of what constitutes worthwhile knowledge, has been abandoned in favour of a curriculum where basic skills and vocational training displace the humanities and creative arts for working-class children. We are in serious danger of establishing a new form of educational apartheid.

It is no easy matter to rethink curriculum in relation to subordinate sections of a divided society, as we have seen in the intense debates surrounding education for a multiethnic society. Initial attempts at a multicultural curriculum which celebrated diversity were rightly condemned as superficial and exotic. More is at stake than increasing the representation of minorities through feasts and photographs, though this cannot be neglected. Our society is marked not only by diversity but by power differences manifested in prejudice, discrimination and institutional racism. Early attempts at an antiracist curriculum properly recognised this, but tended to blame all white people for these problems.

More recent developments in antiracist and multicultural curriculum provide a better response to the interplay of culture and social power, heritage and economics, identity and oppression. We are more aware now of the dynamic complexities of young people's lives, that they do not have a simple identity derived from cultural heritage but are constantly renegotiating and weighing up alternative futures within a forcefield of interlocking oppressions as well as some opportunities.

The difficulties should not, however, deter us from rethinking school curricula in relation to an increasingly insecure and impoverished working-class. I use the term 'working-class' not to fall back on some anachronistic cultural stereotypes. I also wish to put aside, for a moment, the more encompassing Marxist sense in which the vast majority in our society depend on selling their time and their skills – their labour power – to the owners of capital or the means of production. This is an important definition, but, within that larger category, a sub-set is of particular interest for the School Improvement project, namely manual workers and the unemployed. The longstanding issues of educational disaffection for the children of manual workers have been exacerbated by the increasing polarisation between rich and poor in our society, resulting in areas of chronic unemployment and poverty.

Given the high correlation between poverty, limited parental education and underachievement at school, it is fair to suggest that the key policy makers, and some school improvement experts, are in denial. Improvement is scarcely possible unless we consider curriculum change which might make learning more meaningful and empowering to the children who are achieving least through the standard version. Paradoxically, in England, it is now the very schools which are succeeding least with the National Curriculum who have least scope to deviate from it!

> There is no need to remove the national curriculum requirements from successful schools because they are succeeding. Why change things? We have a success. The place where greater freedom is most needed is in those schools which are not succeeding. I tend to believe that the proposal is perverse. (Lord Dearing, May 2002)

Education Action Zones were given a mission to innovate in troubled inner cities, but were then placed under such pressure to meet short-term performance targets that curriculum development was largely abandoned. There have been better models in the past. For example, the gulf between traditional academic curricula and Liverpool's inner city population led Eric Midwinter (1972) to develop a more relevant 'community curriculum' for its Educational Priority Area.

There is a danger that such a curriculum might restrict working-class children to an immediate culture and circumscribe their futures. How can this be avoided? What would a worthwhile curriculum involve for children growing up in poverty? When 19th century socialists were presented with a curriculum of 'useful knowledge' serving industrial needs – the vocationalist option of its day – they declared it lacking and demanded '*really* useful knowledge', knowledge '*concerning our conditions in life . . .* [and] *how to get out of our present troubles*' (in Johnson 1979).

Such a curriculum would include vocational experiences and skills, but also many opportunities to engage with local issues and expand understanding of the global forces which shape our lives.

> Rather than just a study of working-class culture and working-class life [such a curriculum] must be a study of the relations of the working class to the rest of society: the forces by which this relationship is created and sustained, and the ways in which this relationship can be investigated, questioned and eventually transformed. (Ozolins 1979: 50, cited in Whitty 1981)

Cultural respect is vital, but an uncritical reflection of local life-styles would risk condemning the disadvantaged to the ghetto. In a different (postcolonial) context, Burtonwood (1986: 153) argued for a curriculum which opens up new possibilities, for 'culture conflict' as well as 'culture contact', for the curricular potential of the counterculture:

> . . . an education which embraces cognitive change and expansion . . . a curriculum which gives pupils experience in the untamed margins of the world and the mind . . . a vision which is more creative and infinitely more optimistic than the cultural apartheid emanating from the relativism which would deny us access to other worlds. The job of schooling has always been to open windows on to wider worlds. (*ibid*: 154)

The school improvement project needs to move beyond its compliance with an imposed curriculum which manifestly is not working in many schools. The rhetoric of entitlement and common standards need to be re-examined within the reality of a divided and unequal society, and solutions found which genuinely open opportunities to marginalised individuals and communities.

Curriculum and school culture in a changing world

The mismatch between an imposed curriculum and its target audience particularly affects marginalised young people who are little motivated by the promise of jam tomorrow if they would only persist at tasks which appear meaningless today. However, this cultural problem affects a larger group of students, particularly during adolescence.

Youth culture

The drive to improve schools involves youngsters who are themselves cultural constructs. Jane Kenway speaks of the construction of young children as consumers, and the relationships between identity, pleasure and purchase.

You buy delights . . . kids rule . . . adults are dim . . . and schools are dull. These
are the canons of globalizing consumer cultures. In the places where kids,
commodities and images meet, education, entertainment and advertising
merge. Kids consume this corporate abundance with an appetite. Young
people are being turned into 'desiring machines'. (Kenway 2001; see also
Kenway and Bullen 2001)

By contrast, schools are 'pleasure-free zones', because of increased
pressures to deliver results. In this context, the pressures of improvement through target-setting and high-stakes testing are unsustainable –
the promise of 'jam tomorrow' simply will not compete with pleasure
today for many adolescents.

This raises some vital issues. How can we develop forms of learning
which involve personal satisfaction? We cannot simply compete with the
media by providing instant gratification through soundbite flashes of
knowledge, but we must turn schools into learning communities where
young people gain satisfaction from cooperative problem solving and
engagement in activity, and where students write for real audiences
(including each other), not just for a teacher to grade. That means more
flexibility in choosing issues which the students find meaningful, rather
than a constant struggle to cover all the content in the schemes of work

A culture of achievement

Improvement processes are increasingly being examined in terms of
culture. This must extend to investigating the relationship of students to
the curriculum and their own learning. The connection between students
and their curriculum is an important constituent of their 'hidden curriculum'.

This is particularly critical for learners living in poverty, or whose
parents have had a poor experience of education. If these young people
are unconvinced by school learning, if it appears irrelevant to their lives,
if the promise of a good job when they grow up seems too distant and
unlikely, if the hierarchies of school seem too close a replica of the hierarchies they can expect in working life, the situation cannot be 'turned
round' simply by tightening the controls. The transformation of educational culture involves turning round the school in relation to young
people.

This involves a better understanding of the interactions involved in
school learning. Traditionally school work has been a form of *alienated
labour*, rather like production lines in a factory. Borrowing the terminology of Marxist economics (originally from Adam Smith), learning is

seen to have an exchange value, never a use value. You're told what task to do, you perform it for a fixed period of time, you hand over the product, and it receives a mark (a surrogate wage). This reward is increasingly meaningless to you as you grow older – neither it, nor the gold stars or stickers or merit certificates you're promised will buy the things you want. The emphasis on extrinsic rewards as an incentive to improving results needs to be supplemented, if not replaced, by a transformation of school work so that it becomes intrinsically rewarding.

> Creating an achievement culture may mean establishing a strong counter-culture to the street environment, especially for boys. They need to feel a real thrill about their school work, gaining high self-esteem from what they produce there . . .
>
> To create an achievement culture, work of all kinds has to be collectively valued – displayed, read aloud, enacted, sat on, eaten, printed, performed, enjoyed. (Wrigley 2000b: 10–11)

Authorship

The rigidity of a curriculum imposed from outside deeply affects the attitude to learning of a generation accustomed to rapid choice. It is no use arguing that young people's choices are often trivial – the logos on their clothes, channel-hopping on cable TV. Rather than denying choice in schools, we have to engage learners in making wiser choices.

Instead of a rush to cover a large number of specific objectives or an extensive body of content, we need a framework which highlights deeper aims and a smaller number of key concepts. There should be less concern with detailed objectives and more with broader aims and values. This would allow teachers to be more invitational, and to negotiate the choice of topic with their classes. It would create space for learning which engages with issues which are partly generated by the learners, and where students have a degree of *authorship* of the curriculum.

> How can we reconceptualise and reconstruct the curriculum in such a way that pupils, at least for part of the time, have an opportunity for fashioning some time for themselves so that they can pursue their own ideas and studies? (Davies and Edwards 2001: 104)

One model for reconciling an overall structure with a range of student choice can be found in Denmark's social studies curriculum (akin to the emerging Education for Citizenship in Britain) (Ministry of Education, Denmark, 1995). This document provides an architecture which exemplifies how learning can be rigorous as well as relevant and partici-patory. The successive stages involve

(i) learners identifying issues they wish to pursue within a common theme to which they have committed themselves

(ii) teachers connecting social science concepts to experiences raised by learners

(iii) independent and small group research

(iv) a final plenary session which is more than simply reporting back, but involves groups of students organising activities which provoke further discussion and debate.

Recommendations for planning the social studies curriculum in Danish schools

It can be valuable to work out a plan for the year, so that you can order resources in time and organise guest speakers etc., but the plan should consist of broad and open possibilities which give room for adjustments and changes, and not least to encourage and accommodate students' participation and co-responsibility.

Learning can start from a theme, which leads in discussion to the formulation of problems and issues. Alternatively, it can also arise from questions and issues which students themselves have brought to class. In this case, the students and teacher need to consider which theme will provide a framework for these issues or problems. In either case, use will be made of some social science methods or concepts.

*   *   *

In the final stage, the results may take the form of reports, folders, posters etc. but they're not always a physical product. The students might produce their results as a talk, a drama or a simulation game, leading to discussion. This stage has great importance and isn't just a closure to the learning process. The learners should be clear that they may not be able to reach final conclusions, and that they're reaching provisional answers. The final stage also involves an evaluation by students and the teacher of the entire learning process.

(Ministry of Education, Denmark 1995)

Breadth and balance?

A wider understanding of achievement also needs to underpin the improvement project. This is not to suggest that students from working-class or minority backgrounds do not need examination success; they need it more than anyone, as a passport towards future opportunities, an objective demonstration of achievement which may partly overcome discrimination in gaining employment or entry to university. Nevertheless, examination results in themselves are simply not enough.

In chapter 2, in the context of bilingual learners of South Asian origin, I argued for a broad definition of achievement to include cultural and political learning, social and moral engagement, and intercultural understanding. We need to work at a similar definition for – no, *with* – other working-class communities. Improvement is not something that can be done *to* people.

It is questionable whether authentic learning can ever develop within a curriculum which is assessed in traditional ways. This is a key improvement issue. Do our modes of assessment – the very device whereby we evaluate and drive school improvement – actually undermine real learning? A Scottish exchange student, after two days in a progressive secondary school in Germany, expressed the difference wonderfully:

> Here, school's about *learning*. Back home, it's just about *passing*.

Assessment conveys deep messages to students about learning. The shift from norm-referencing to criterion-referencing has not achieved its desired result. The traditional norm-referencing placed children in rank order, gave them grades, and declared a proportion to have failed. The hybrid system now used in Britain (a ladder of criterion-referenced steps) leaves intact a sense of learning hierarchies, fixed obstacles to overcome, and children who have failed. It might have worked very differently – as a set of aspirational targets against which individual children strive for their personal best – but for the setting of national targets and crucial barriers (e.g. increasing to 80 per cent the proportion of children reaching Level 4 at the end of Key Stage 2). Recent research shows the greater effectiveness of assessment as feedback, when work is returned to pupils with comments and advice but normally without marks, grades or levels (Black *et al* 2002).

Accountability and target-setting is leading to a trivialisation of learning. We need neither a return to the irrelevant high-level demands of the traditional academic curriculum, nor a 'progressive' absence of rigour, but rather a spotlight on the high-level demands of *critical engagement*.

This would involve what is commonly referred to as thinking skills but goes beyond it into a personal and collective engagement with real issues.

The metacurriculum of thinking

The vast expansion of knowledge, and its easier availability through information technology, require greater emphasis on thinking processes. Serious attention is being paid to a range of initiatives and models, from Thinking Skills programmes independent of specific curricula, through Children's Philosophy models rooted in narratives, to models closely related to specific subjects such as Cognitive Acceleration in Science Education (CASE) and related projects.

In *Smart Schools*, David Perkins emphasises 'knowledge about knowledge' or *meta*cognition. Examples include familiarity with ideas such as hypothesis and evidence, general problem-solving strategies, and an understanding about what evidence is like in different disciplines (e.g. formal proof in mathematics, experiment in science, argument from the text and from historical context in literature). He proposes giving more lesson time to metacognitive challenges:

> What do you do when you don't understand something if you want to understand it better? For example, what would you do if you wanted to understand something like Abraham Lincoln's Gettysburg Address, long division, or a suit of armor, just by thinking about it? What questions would you ask yourself about it? (Perkins 1992: 99)

Perkins suggests the following strategies for creating the *metacurriculum*, all of which can be incorporated into a content curriculum more successfully than by creating a separate Thinking Skills course:

- making more deliberate use of cognitive terms such as hypothesis, predict, contradictions

- challenging loose statements in everyday conversation such as 'Everybody has one', or 'This cereal is more nutritious'. (The teacher might ask 'Who exactly?' or 'More nutritious than what?')

- 'thinking on paper', or trying to represent an idea diagramatically as it emerges

- developing a passion for intellectual curiosity

- exploring similarities and differences between historical events or scientific phenomena, in order to generate larger concepts. (*ibid*: 107–119)

Teaching the metacurriculum within a course on the American Constitution

• Thinking about the design of the document (the purpose of the preamble, its inspirational tone, etc.)

• Examining the rhetorical devices ('We the People', which covers up the extent of disagreement at the time, and the fact that the majority were disenfranchised)

• What evidence it is possible to have about how people really thought in the past

• Comparisons with other documents such as the Declaration of Independence and Magna Carta ('documents that have set nations upon a path')

• Asking whether the school has a constitution, and what it should contain.

(Perkins 1992: 128–130)

I found similar attention to cognitive processes and deep concepts in curriculum planning at Plashet School, in the East End of London, a school with very high achievement levels despite extreme poverty in the area. This resulted from close cooperation between language develop-ment (EAL) teachers and the subject specialists. In history for example, deeper level concepts were identified which could be taught from a parti-cular example. This included not only specific concepts (e.g. words such as bishops, pope, heaven and hell when studying medieval Christianity) but more fundamental concepts (hierarchy, social control) and historical processes (e.g. interpreting from images and literary texts). Each unit involved a key activity designed to engage students emotionally, linguis-tically and cognitively, for example drawing posters on heaven and hell based on Dante's *Inferno*, or writing a job description and interviewing candidates for the post of parish priest in a medieval village. (Wrigley 2000: 70–73)

Superficial breadth or deeper understandings: 'essential' schools

The Coalition of Essential Schools (USA) is based on Theodore Sizer's belief that deeper thinking is more important than extensive content coverage. Each school joining the Coalition develops differently, but based on a few common principles and with extensive mutual support and learning. In Central Park East secondary school in New York, most teaching is divided into two broad areas, humanities and mathematics/

science. Within these areas, different specialists work together but with limits on the number of teachers each student will be taught by. The central manifesto for learning, The Promise, sets expectations for students and teachers to deepen learning in whatever they pursue. In each project, students are guided by five core questions:

- *Viewpoint*: From whose viewpoint are we hearing this? to who's speaking? Would this look different if she or he were in another place or time?

- *Evidence*: How do we know what we know? What evidence will we accept? How credible will such evidence appear to others? What rules of evidence are appropriate to different tasks?

- *Connections and patterns*: How are things connected together? Have we ever encountered this before? Is there a discernible pattern here? What came first? Is there a clear cause and efffect? What are the probable consequences that might follow from taking course x rather than course y? How probable? Is this a 'law' of causality, a probability, or a mere correlation?

- *Conjecture*: What if things had been different? Suppose King George had been a very different personality? Suppose Napoleon or Martin Luther King Jr or Hitler had not been born? Suppose King's assassin had missed? (Our fourth habit encompassed our belief that a well educated person saw alternatives, other possibilities, and assumed that choices mattered. They could make a difference. The future wasn't, perhaps, inevitable.)

- And finally – who, after all, cares? Does it *matter*? And to whom? Is it of mere 'academic' interest, or might it lead to significant *changes* in the way we see the world and the world sees us? Will it make us richer? More famous? More powerful? Can we know? (from Debbie Meier 1998: 607–8)

Into the future

We have a very limited awareness of educational futures, and all too often computer technology appears as a universal panacea. Not that information technologies are unimportant, but that it is only one of the issues which should be shaping our thinking about future schools.

The state of Queensland, Australia is running a pilot project *New Basics* to develop a curriculum for the future (see *Education Queensland* website). Allan Luke outlines some core issues:

(i) *New youth cultures*

New identities, new ways of growing up, new ways of learning, and so on. The problem is, 'These kids are not like us'.

Globalisation is leading to the emergence of world kids, post-modern kids who learn and behave differently – and we baby-boomers are struggling with how to deal with this – often attempting to draw them back into a nostalgic past.

New cultural contexts and identities are leading to multilingual and multicultural populations, cultural hybridity, new types of popular cultural texts, and new cultural identities.

(ii) *New fields of discipline and knowledge*

The problem is not just about the knowledge explosion, but the difficulty we have dealing with whole new, often melded domains. Disciplines never are what they used to be, except in high schools.

(iii) *Persistent patterns of inequality*

With the development of the knowledge economy, the old economy and class divide does not disappear.

Global economies are changing communities: semiotic/information economies; structural unemployment; contracts, out-sourcing and sub-contracting; service and information 'McJobs'; retrainability and educability.

(iv) *The 'unfinished business of nation building'*

Issues that are vexing Australia at the moment: our national identity crisis over our place in the Asia/Pacific, the variable kinds of control we have over flows of culture/knowledge/bodies across boundaries and borders, the unfinished business of Reconciliation [the Aboriginal population], our analysis of the sustainability of our place on this land and on this planet, and the kinds of social and economic issues raised by new economies and divisions of wealth in this milieu. (Luke 2001)

Luke's fourth point, from an Australian perspective, illustrates how different globalisation looks from different places on the planet. Together, the four points establish a more thoughtful foundation for curriculum reform than an obsession with ICT.

Luke argues against the disempowering and deprofessionalising effects of a curriculum focused on accountability and high-stakes testing. He is opposed to just adding on programs, or a 'wires and boxes approach where we put the technology in with the hope that it will then all be OK'. The project seeks to align the New Basics curriculum framework, Productive Pedagogies and a new form of assessment known as Rich Tasks.

> The New Basics are futures-oriented categories for organising curriculum . . . clusters of essential practices that students need in order to flourish in 'new times' . . . There are four New Basics organisers and they have an explicit orientation towards researching, understanding, and coming to grips with the new economic, cultural and social conditions. These four clusters of practice are deemed to be essential for lifelong learning by the individual, for social cohesion, and for economic wellbeing. (Education Queensland 2000: New Basics)

Individual schools are responsible for choosing how to organise time and teacher responsibilities, but are recommended to emphasise connectedness, teamwork and, for secondary schools, a limited number of teachers working with students, for example:

> *Primary*: a team of three teachers in Years 4, 5 and 6 could plan a three-year curriculum programme while maintaining their traditional classroom organisation
>
> *Secondary*: teams of five or six teachers work together with a group of students over a two-year period.

Transdisciplinary work in the New Basics project does not abandon academic disciplines, but requires a creative reconnection and reconstruction which will draw upon the knowledge and talents of teachers from different specialisms.

The rich tasks are a radically different form of evaluation and accountability from normal tests and exams. A rich task is:

> a culminating performance or demonstration or product that is *purposeful* and *models a life role*. It presents *substantive, real problems* and engages learners in forms of pragmatic social action that have *real value in the world*. The problems require identification, analysis and resolution . . . Tasks *connect to the world outside the classroom*.

Intensification or improvement?

School improvement for the 21st century requires more than just an efficiency drive, or even an advanced understanding of change processes. In such a time of change as ours, this requires a rethinking of curriculum, its aims and content, and its relationship to teaching and assessment.

The literature of school improvement is clear on the need for ownership of the change process, but this sense of ownership is equally important for the curriculum. We face at present a debilitating contradiction between an imposed curriculum and the encouragement for schools to take responsibility for change.

Teachers and students need to recover a sense of *authorship and creativity*. This is not to propose an individualistic model, nor to deny the importance of wider frameworks beyond the single school. Broadly defined frameworks can be drawn up which allow ample space for local decision-making, with peer support and collaboration across a region or network. Curriculum development networks have the potential for significantly raising achievement, and already have some proven success.

The School Improvement project needs to grasp the nettle of curriculum design, in relation to a rapidly changing world but also in terms of the deep divisions within that world, globally and locally. This is not simply a matter of finding more efficient curriculum structures, but of opportunities which empower tomorrow's citizens towards democratic control of their troubled environment. In place of the curriculum of the dead, we need to launch a debate about a curriculum of hope.

Education Queensland: the New Basics

Life pathways and social futures: who am I and where am I going?
- living in and preparing for diverse family relationships
- collaborating with peers and others
- maintaining health and care of the self
- learning about and preparing for new worlds of work
- developing initiative and enterprise.

Multiliteracies and communications media: how do I make sense of and communicate with the world?

'Technologies of communication that use various codes for the exchange of messages, texts and information', including
- spoken language, writing and print
- visual media like photograph and film
- television and digital information technologies
- mathematics
- community and foreign languages and intercultural understanding
- the creative and performing arts.

Active citizenship: what are my rights and responsibilities in communities, cultures and economies?
- interacting within local and global communities
- operating within shifting cultural identities
- understanding local and global economic forces
- understanding the historical foundation of social movements and civic institutions.

Environments and technologies: how do I describe, analyse and shape the world around me?

An opportunity to 'examine and interact critically with the physical world'. It contextualises scientific understanding, and makes connections between science and technology and social, cultural, economic, environmental and ethical issues.

- developing a scientific understanding of the world
- working with design and engineering technologies
- building and sustaining environments.

CHAPTER SEVEN

Pedagogies for improving schools

*Why is it, in spite of the fact that teaching by pouring in, learning by a
passive absorption, are universally condemned, that they are still so
entrenched in practice? That education is not an affair of 'telling' and
being told but an active and constructive process, is a principle almost as
generally violated in practice as conceded in theory.*

(John Dewey, 1916)

*In times of change, the learners will inherit the earth, while the knowers
will find themselves beautifully equipped to deal with a world that no
longer exists.*

(Eric Hoffer)

Education cannot survive long without hope. It would stop altogether in
a society which lost all hope for the future.

The 20th century saw repeated attempts to found a science of teaching –
in the sense that teaching might be reduced to a set of objective laws, a
collection of recordable behaviours. For those who seek to unravel the
mysteries of teaching in terms of the amount of time on task, the pace of
instruction, or the accuracy of the assessment record, I suggest a different
starting point – a sense of future. It's not that good teaching cannot be
explained, but rather that our explanations need to be articulated in more
holistic and ethical terms.

This places a question mark on much of the teaching we find in schools.
If, as Freire suggests, dialogue depends on hope, then why do we find so
little that resembles true dialogue in classrooms? If learning has the
potential to offer us alternative futures, why does school learning so often
feel like a transfer of *inert* knowledge?

There is renewed emphasis on the classroom level in the School
Improvement literature and a recognition that unless whole-school
change is paralleled by a focus on learning and teaching, it is unlikely to

have much impact on achievement. But this is insufficient as the basis for developing a new agenda for School Improvement, and can lead to an indiscriminate adoption of more 'efficient' teaching methods which do not cohere with each other, with the direction of whole-school change or wider social transformation. The improvement of learning needs to be understood as part of a broader ethical project. The present chapter gives some pointers, and particularly relates the promotion of higher cognitive levels with the democratisation of learning and with a greater connectedness between cognitive, affective and practical development. (See for example the use of the words *Bildung* and *Pädagogik* in the German tradition.)

We are not the first generation to wish to bring new life to learning. Socrates, Comenius, Rousseau, Dewey and many others have questioned the formalised learning of their day, and tried to do things better. Periods of educational reform have often coincided with great turning points in history, and have invariably begun as the movement of a minority, opposed by the dominant forces of their day. Educational history brings many surprises. I read the other day of the school attended by John Keats, founded by John Ryland. Its teachers were religious non-conformists associated with the most daring scientists and democratic radicals of the day, the age of the French and American Revolutions.

> One autumn morning, John Ryland called up the whole school to see the departure of the swallows, which had clustered in surprising numbers on the roof of the building . . .
>
> Ryland, who believed in educating his pupils 'by recreation', would demon-strate the movements of planets and moons in the solar system . . . in the playground. Individual pupils were given a card identifying one of the planets or a moon, and listing some information to be learnt. With their cards, the pupil-planets and moons took up their stations in an appropriate circle of orbit around the classmate representing 'the great Sun'. The 'living orrery' was then set in motion. (Roe 1997: 29–36)

This live engagement with the world, combining head, heart and hand, is infinitely more advanced than the supposedly scientific explanations of teaching of the positivist era. Starting around 1920, the controlling forces in American education set out to define learning in terms of thousands of specific objectives. It was like pinning down a butterfly – they just don't fly after that. Through hundreds of studies of 'effective instruction', teaching as the transmission of fragmentary facts and sub-skills was subjected to structured observation and quantitative analysis in the attempt to isolate teacher behaviours which would lead to the most efficient acquisition. The butterfly still won't fly. In the last quarter century, this Fordist mass production of knowledge has literally been tested to destruction; the efficiency of teachers in transferring the set information into children's minds has been increasingly regulated through a regime of high stakes testing.

Among its many critics, here is John Taylor Gatto, in his provocative book *Dumbing Us Down*. (It should be noted that these are not the sour grapes of a 'failing teacher'; Gatto had won numerous awards, including New York State Teacher of the Year after 25 years of successful inner-city teaching.)

> The first lesson I teach is confusion. Everything I teach is out of context . . . I teach dis-connections . . .
>
> The logic of the school-mind is that it is better to leave school with a tool kit of superficial jargon derived from economics, sociology, natural science, and so on, than with one genuine enthusiasm. But quality in education entails learning about something in depth . . .
>
> I teach the un-relating of everything, an infinite fragmentation the opposite of cohesion; what I do is more related to television programming than to making a scheme of order . . . I teach you how to accept confusion as your destiny. That's the first lesson I teach. (1992: 2–4)

Positivism, inspection, and effectiveness research

Effectiveness research is dogmatically untheoretical in its study of teaching. Much of it seeks an explanation in terms of quantity, such as time on task, frequency of questions, or highly visible and easily recorded surface features such as classroom layout or specific pupil behaviours. (This is evident, for example, in the literature review by Sammons *et al* 1995.) There is little attempt in this literature to analyse interactions in terms of cognitive processes, and no clear foundation in a theory of pedagogy. In places, they warn against too simplistic a quantitative perspective:

> As Carroll (1989) cautioned 'time as such is not what counts, but what happens during that time' (Sammons et al 1995: 14)

At times, a pedagogical theory is implicit (Ausubel's 'advance organiser'?):

> Effective learning occurs where teachers clearly explain the objectives of the lesson at the outset. (*ibid*: 16)

In the main, however, we see recommendations for the intensification of surface features of teacher performance: 'Keep the teaching sessions task-oriented' or 'Have high expectations for achievement (give more homework, pace lessons faster, create alertness)'.

Such a thin and untheorized account was adopted for lesson observation by the English inspection agency Ofsted, which is why its inspection reports strip lessons bare of their real strength and shape, making it impossible for readers to imagine what happened or relate them to their own experience and sense of purpose. Inspectors have to use discrete observable categories: pace, planning, assessment, homework, use of resources and experiences. Teaching Methods is just another item on the list, with no guiding principle of what quality might consist of other than a 'variety' of 'appropriate' methods.

This discourse looks at teaching mechanistically, as a set of external behaviours which are not linked to a view of learning. It is a catalogue of teacher performances, rather than a pattern of meaningful interactions between teachers and learners.

> Simple solutions for improving teaching . . . often focus on individual features of teaching, such as using concrete materials, asking higher-order questions, or forming cooperative groups. But teaching is not just a collection of individual features. It is a system composed of tightly connected elements. And the system is rooted in deep-seated beliefs about the nature of the subject, the way students learn, and the role of the teacher. (Stigler and Hiebert 1999: 8)

Hiebert and Stigler's research digs below the surface of teacher behaviours to look at the quality of *reasoning* in mathematics lessons. Deductive reasoning – the reasoning needed to draw logical conclusions from premises – was found in 62 per cent of the Japanese lessons and 0 per cent of the American sample. (*ibid*: 4)

The Japanese teachers place high demands on the learners' problem-solving abilities, and simultaneously empower them as agents in their own learning. They give students time to struggle with challenging problems before providing direct explanations and summaries of what the students have learned. Whole-class teaching has a different role in the USA and Japan. In American classrooms it normally *precedes individual practice*: the teacher demonstrates how to solve a sample problem, clarifies the steps of a fixed algorithm which the students then apply to numerous examples. In the Japanese classrooms, direct teaching *follows group discussion*. The problem is usually 'one that students do not know how to solve immediately but for which they have learned some crucial concepts or procedures in their previous lessons. Students are asked to work on the problem for a specified number of minutes and then to share their solutions.' (*ibid*: 6–7)

American students spend most of their time acquiring isolated skills through repeated practice . . . irrespective of whether students are working individually in rows or are sitting in groups, or whether they are using pencil and paper or have access to the latest technology. (Hopkins 2001: 79)

Improving schools through 'direct' instruction?

The repeated advice from government agencies in England has been: more direct teaching. This would be unproblematic if pupils really were empty containers into which knowledge could be poured. Constructivist theories of learning, on the other hand, emphasise the need for learners to process information for themselves.

A transmission model, whereby teachers project a stream of facts and sub-skills, produces learning as *replication* – pupils copy down information and later demonstrate their knowledge by regurgitating what they have learnt through essays, practice examples and tests. This is such a long-established tradition that teaching and learning tend to collapse back into it by default if we don't deliberately set out to do things differently.

This is not to suggest that direct teaching is always inappropriate, but it has to involve ways of activating the learner's attention – sometimes known as 'direct interactive teaching'. Whole-class teaching, and even lectures to a larger audience, can be redesigned to subvert assumptions of learner subservience and passivity. This is necessary in order to raise the cognitive level and connect symbolic processing with feelings, action and experience.

Perkins suggests

• eliciting further examples

• asking learners to compare local examples with more distant ones

• analysing what they see

• linking new concepts to old

• and testing out new ideas by means of principles they already know. (1992: 54)

He recommends we avoid simple replication in learning by requiring students to engage in 'understanding performances'; the learners don't simply demonstrate that they *possess* knowledge but must do things with it and move beyond the information given. This might involve

- explaining something in your own words

- giving new examples

- applying a theory to a phenomenon not yet studied

- or justifying a hypothesis through appropriate evidence. (*ibid*: 77)

Modes of teaching

In order to strike a good balance, beginner teachers in Scotland are asked to consider four 'modes' of teaching: exposition, discussion, enquiry and action learning. They are recommended to avoid an excess of exposition/direct teaching. It is a start but rather too simple: it avoids issues of sequencing, context, purpose and above all, quality of learning. It also neglects the importance of questioning teacher dominance in directing and evaluating learning, and the need to promote students' awareness and evaluation of the aims and success of activities in which they are engaged.

Just as direct teaching can be enhanced by making it more interactive, the other categories can easily be found in debased forms.

- A teacher might describe a lesson as discussion though, to any observer, it looks as if one dominant individual (the teacher) is putting a series of closed questions to younger and less powerful listeners, or occasionally seeking out opinions which more or less coincide with the teacher's own. There is little communication among the learners, who rarely extend or comment upon each others' views.

- Enquiry quickly becomes another form of replication learning in which the individual pupil copies extracts from a reference book. When the teacher advises them to 'put it in your own words', the pupils understand this simply as a requirement to omit a few verbs and articles.

- Action learning can become thoughtless activity, in which pupils copy an artistic technique or carry out a science experiment which has been entirely designed by the teacher and whose conclusion is already obvious.

In any mode, we need to deliberately subvert replication learning. To enhance learning and retain new knowledge in memory, we need to engage the learner's mind in actively processing the information in some way. We have to be constantly alert to routinised activities which do not result in real understanding.

A particular example would be the frequent use of 'comprehensions' in a variety of subjects. This type of activity perhaps owes its popularity among teachers to its incorporation of testing and control into teaching, but it is questionable as a means of developing understanding. It has been shown that pupils can answer questions without actually understanding the text, simply by transforming the syntax and paying attention to the order of words. The following extract from a nonsense passage shows how this works:

The Blonke

This particular blonke was quite drumly – lennow, in fact, and almost samded. When yerden, it did not quetch like the other blonkes, or even blore. The others blored very readily.

Q1 What is 'drumly'?

Q2 In what way(s) was the drumly blonke unlike the others?

(from Simons, ed: *The English Curriculum – Comprehension*)

A more dynamic engagement would require us to *do something* with a text, such as:

• predicting how a story will continue

• re-arranging jumbled paragraphs in a narrative or report

• disputing a statement, from someone else's point of view

• comparing two texts on a similar subject

• examining the rhetorical devices used in a newspaper article.

Converting textual information into diagrammatic form encourages a more holistic reading. If our reading begins by asking ourselves what we already know about a topic and what we most want to find out, we become more focused and often more critical readers.

The visual representation of an idea can also be used formatively, during an investigation or in pursuit of an hypothesis. Sometimes we can appreciate a theory or concept more holistically through a visual model than through words alone. (Einstein explained that the idea of relativity first came to him as a mental image – he pictured himself travelling alongside a beam of light!)

Patterns of communication

Schools are verbally saturated, but often in ways which discourage learners from using language to generate their own thinking. There is a different balance between words and actions in schools than elsewhere: an apprentice learning a skill does not defer action until he has heard extended verbal advice or explicit instructions. One of the best technology teachers I have seen avoided lengthy step-by-step explanations at the start of a lesson, but as soon as a pupil asked for help, he would *invite* others to see it demonstrated. A small group would gather round, and listen with full attention because the time was right for them.

Research into classroom discourse shows extreme asymmetry between teacher and learners. The 16th-century French satirist Rabelais challenged the Jesuits' pedagogical methods, asking 'Shouldn't it be the pupils who ask the questions?' We have grown so used to teachers asking all the questions that we fail to notice, but surely it is surprising that four-year-olds who ask their parents a question a minute turn into inarticulate seven-year-olds who in some cases ask their teachers only a few questions a week – usually 'Can I borrow the felt tips? or 'Please miss, may I go to the toilet?' Barnes (1969: 22–3) points out the predominance of factual over reasoning questions, and that genuinely 'open' questions hardly ever occur.

Whereas Freire spoke of true dialogue which is based on hope, our classrooms are so often filled with asymmetrical exchanges that they are almost monologic. The learners use language not to exchange ideas but to show what they have remembered and to prove that they are listening.

Freire associates true dialogue with 'love, hope and mutual trust'. The two parties have a relation of empathy, and are engaged in a joint search. He contrasts this with an 'anti-dialogue' based on hierarchy and control:

> This anti-dialogue does not communicate, but rather issues communiqués. (Freire 1974: 46)

In re-reading his accounts of rural education in Brazil, it is remarkable how closely his description matches what still happens in too many urban classrooms today.

To develop our schools into places for democratic and hopeful learning, we need to transform patterns of communication to open up spaces for learners to contribute actively to the construction of understanding. This requires as radical a rethinking as Freire engaged in for popular education in Brazil. We cannot simply transfer his model, but there is much to learn.

In this rigid, vertical structure of relationships there is no real room for dialogue . . . This is the consciousness of the oppressed. With no experience of dialogue, with no experience of participation, the oppressed are often unsure of themselves. They have consistently been denied their right to have their say, having historically had the duty to only listen and obey . . .

It is a pattern which is hard to break at first: They say to the educator: 'Excuse us, sir, we who don't know should keep quiet and listen to you who know.'

True communication is not, in my opinion, the exclusive transfer or transmission of knoweldge from one Subject to another, but rather his co-participation in the act of comprehending the object. It is communication carried out in a critical way. (Freire 1974: 118–9, 138)

Douglas Barnes' research in the 1970s has lasting relevance for the School Improvement project. Barnes discovered that children are often more articulate in small groups than in the whole-class setting. Sometimes the dialogue is difficult to analyse; it can be messy – the children take over from each other mid sentence, build upon each other's ideas, and make rather tentative half-formed suggestions – but this is a strength, not a weakness. It reflects a cooperative thinking process, the exercise of a shared intelligence, or in Perkins' words, 'distributed cognition'. Terry Phillips (1985) discovered that children in small group activities tend to use two very important forms of language which rarely occur in whole-class situations:

(i) they form hypotheses

(ii) they relate academic theories to everyday experiences.

In response to Bernstein's concept of working-class 'language deficit', critics such as Cooper (1976) have suggested that it might be the language patterns of school which are deficient. The gulf between everyday language and school language is deep and unbridged. Sometimes ideas are rejected because they are expressed in the wrong register.

In a science lesson, pupils were shown pictures of a foetus in a womb. One boy asked: 'How does it go to the toilet?' This is a sensible question and shows that the pupil is thinking for himself. The teacher ignored the questions, commenting later 'He must have been joking.' (Keddie 1971, in Stubbs 1983: 18)

When children transfer to secondary school, they quickly learn that their everyday knowledge has no place within the academic discourse of subject specialists. Their attempts to exemplify or test out teachers' theories in terms of their own experience and observations are overlooked or regarded as distractions, especially when the teacher feels under pressure to cover the syllabus. (See, for example, Barnes 1969: 28) The pressure to learn a new code – the passive voice in science, an objective unconcerned tone in history – can be so great that pupils' own voices are smothered – and especially for working class or ethnic minority pupils who are less comfortable with formal academic registers. Messages are unconsciously given out that pupils' families and communities, their lives out of school, their language and experiences are of no account to the school – an important though neglected issue for School Improvement's research into culture and ethos.

Developing cognition

Piaget's theory of child development links levels of cognitive activity to chronological age. This was challenged by Vygotsky, who regarded development as potentially more dynamic if the teacher responds to the learners' existing understanding and engages with them in a sympathetic but challenging dialogue.

According to Piaget, children reach a stage of abstract reasoning around the age of 11. Michael Shayer and Philip Adey (1981), replicating Piaget's research, concluded that the majority of inner city pupils haven't achieved this independently by the age of 14 or even 16. Rather than becoming demoralised or concluding that comprehensive schools are a futile utopian dream, they set out to understand the conditions under which cognitive development could be accelerated by bridging the gap between concrete operational and formal operational thinking. Thus began the CASE (Cognitive Acceleration in Science Education) project, and similar initiatives in other subjects.

The provocative title *Really Raising Standards* (Adey and Shayer, 1994) threw down a gauntlet to improvement specialists who, at that time, were largely ignoring pedagogical theory while focusing exclusively on whole-school management. Based on constructivist psychology, Adey and Shayer identify five key elements of a pedagogy to develop cognition:

(i)   concrete preparation

(ii) cognitive conflict

(iii) construction zone activity

(iv) metacognition

(v) bridging.

Concrete Preparation entails both rich experience and introduction to a specialist vocabulary. Cognitive Conflict describes an event or observation which the student finds puzzling, and discordant with previous experience or understanding. Construction Zone Activity is mental activity which is speculative and collaborative:

> a magic place where minds meet, where things are not the same to all who see them, where meanings are fluid, and where one person's construal may preempt another's.

Metacognition involves not only a personal control over the activity, but self-reflection and higher-level modelling on the part of the learner. Bridging is the conscious transfer of a theory to new situations and problems.

The benefits of this method include:

• linking school learning back into direct experience

• connecting words with meanings

• providing the opportunity for students to engage in exploratory dialogue

• giving them a conscious control over the learning process

• then taking the ideas forward into new situations and problems.

It shows a respect for learners and an active hope for their future development.

When visiting case study schools for *The Power to Learn* (Wrigley 2000*)*, I saw many examples of similar practices. Teachers of bilingual students were conscious of the need to contextualise learning in first-hand experience. They sought to establish the subject vocabulary by relating it to direct experience, rather than simply displaying definitions of *key words*. They understood the importance of fieldwork, video, and tactile and visual experience.

Problems were posed in a manner which was rich in language and experience. Students who were studying evolution drew imaginary islands, each with a distinct climate and vegetation. The teacher placed an unsuitable animal into this habitat, provoking a discussion on how it might survive. Pupils then went on to discuss how it might adapt.

Construction zone activity was carefully planned. In a study of population changes, students discussed where to place narrative statements of events on a graph (see Leat 1998). Students studying the English Civil War sorted role-cards of a family into those who would support the King or Parliament, then engaged in a simulation of the family's heated debate over dinner. Focusing on a shared problem, learners were able to shift easily between personal memory, immediate experience, visual representation and words. Pupils working in small groups are more likely to refer to their personal experience and to form hypotheses. Collaborative group work provides a context for bridging the gap between everyday language and the more formal academic register of schooling.

The development of metacognition depends on thoughtful planning. It has become standard practice for teachers to point out the key words of a particular topic, but identifying deeper concepts and processes is less common. For science Adey and Shayer (1994: 82) have identified central concepts such as classification, variables, correlation and equilibrium; for geography, Leat (1998) suggests classification, location, systems, inequality and development. I saw good examples of classes being asked to reflect on the learning process by thinking about core concepts or discussing the proposed method of investigation or the nature of proof. In a lesson about bacteria, pupils were encouraged to design alternative experiments to explore their hypotheses about the best conditions for reproduction.

By successfully linking between concrete and abstract, specific and general, the familiar and the academic, teachers skilfully prepared the ground for bridging ideas into new contexts. Pupils were invited to suggest new applications for the theories they had learnt.

Multiple intelligences in practice

Our school tradition places extraordinary emphasis on verbal communication. Exposition combined with questions is the prime form of teaching, and writing the means of demonstrating what you have learnt. Primary school children soon understand that the chief way to show you understand is to write about it, and, implicitly, that poor writing skills means a lack of intelligence. This is often a critical problem for students from working class and ethnic minority backgrounds, and may be particularly affected by the slower maturation of boys.

Through his concept of multiple intelligences, Howard Gardner (1993) makes it more difficult to assume that some children are simply incapable, and challenges educators to find new routes to successful learning.

The Children's University and the University of the First Age, founded in Birmingham for primary and secondary pupils, have a particular interest in exploring diverse sensory channels and forms of representation. This can be be seen not only at the universities' special events, but also in schools through superlearning days which make a highly creative use of the concept of multiple intelligences. In Golden Hillock School, Birmingham, a class of 14-year-olds were having difficulty distinguishing between the message of a text and the style used to convey that message. The teacher switched from studying the book *War of the Worlds* to watching the film *Startrek Insurrection* to explore how particular techniques, within a genre, are used to suggest ideas to the audience. They discussed dramatic shifts in the music, the images of a blissful rural community (children playing, mothers baking bread), the use of camera angles to engender fear, the cliched semiotics of good and evil, innocence and villainy. They recalled the music in *Jaws* and various horror films (Wrigley 2000: 139).

Many primary school teachers are concerned that the literacy hour tends to divorce the written from the spoken word and from experience. Two teachers in Whetley Primary School, Bradford, worked hard to reinforce such links wherever possible. On one wall, a giant map had been painted of a remote Scottish island, based on the story of *Katy Morag and the two grandmothers*; on the opposite wall was a map of Bradford, with many photos taken on class visits. In another classroom, the teacher was using a newspaper report which she had written about the Loch Ness Monster. These young Asian pupils were struggling to understand the origins of an eyewitness-quotation. Some suggested the teacher-as-reporter had found the news in the library, or seen it on television, until one boy realised she might have interviewed someone at the Loch. The teacher quickly switched to a role-play in which this boy played the eye-witness and the others the reporters, using glue-pens as microphones. This developed spoken language, but also interpersonal and intra-personal intelligence. By this means, the two-dimensional text was unpacked and transformed into the four dimensions of time and space. Creative and performing arts had a prominent place throughout the school, and visual and dramatic activities were frequently used across the curriculum (Wrigley 2000: 115).

Gardner's current work, as part of Harvard University's Project Zero team, provides further illumination. He is now building on his multiple intelligences insight by connecting it with the concept of *situated learning*. This has the potential to transform teachers' understanding of the relationship between symbolic representations and participation in activities, and to question the patterns of teacher dominance in classroom learning.

'Learning is something you do to children'

This ironic comment from one teacher sums up some of the pedagogical issues for a dominant mode of school improvement. Traditional styles of teaching as transmission have been reinforced by the accountability regime, leading to high-pressure injection of inert knowledge, rather than active engagement of the learner. Caroline Lodge argues that the learning process is seriously affected by our ways of referring to it.

Her research reveals two major discourses among both pupils and teachers: learning as *work*, and learning as *performance* (Lodge 2002). Learning as performance is focused on 'getting ticks, putting more in your head, pleasing the teacher'. For those who see learning as work, the prime focus is on task completion, and improvement is seen as doing *more*. Both perceptions affect the learner's concept of what it means to improve, which is why so many attempts to involve pupils in evaluating or redrafting their own work have limited success.

An alternative discourse drawing on 'richer and more complex models of learning could be discerned struggling against the more dominant discourses. The rich discourse of learning is relational, post-structural, organic and draws on narratives.' Its key features are:

- *connectivity*: the ability to make connections between one's learning, previous learning, the learning of others and learning in other contexts
- *learner responsibility*: the capacity to negotiate the curriculum, to plan, organise and review their progress and set new goals
- *collaborative learning*: the ability to take different roles in collaborative activities, and to develop new understandings from dialogue
- *activity in learning*: the ability to engage in a variety of learning tasks through active engagement with others, learning resources and processes
- *meta-learning*: knowledge of a range of strategies, the ability to reflect, monitor, evaluate and plan different approaches. (Lodge 2002: 23)

Most students tend to see learning as:

- getting more knowledge
- memorising and reproducing
- applying facts or procedures.

Only a few see it as:

* understanding

* seeing something in a different way, and

* changing as a person (Marton *et al*, 1993).

These last three descriptors represent deeper learning – making meaning, interpreting events and constructing knowledge or understanding.

The dominant discourses of *work* and *performance* favour learners being seated, isolated, silent and writing. Pupils counterpose 'sitting down and writing' to more active forms of learning:

> We're not sitting at tables and writing. You can talk and that.

Their preferred learning involves social interactions, which partly explains why it is seen as advantageous.

The pressures to get work completed can contradict quality. Teachers are driven to set deadlines and push for a greater quantity of neater and more accurate writing, and few students interviewed thought of improving the quality of their work in terms of the quality of thinking or concentration.

School improvement: a new focus on learning

A surprising feature of most of the early literature on school improvement was its virtual neglect of teaching and learning. Although teaching is mentioned in almost every list of Key Characteristics of more successful schools, the literature has been virtually devoid of either description or theory. This was probably inevitable, in the late 1980s and early 1990s, given a new emphasis on the importance of whole-school factors. This has recently been changing.

A good example is Bruce Joyce and Emily Calhoun's collaboration with David Hopkins; together they have produced two companion volumes, one focusing mainly on pedagogy (1997) and the other on school development (1999). However, there is still a lack of coherence in this approach, as the models presented in the former volume constitute separate patterns to be learnt and are not sufficiently related to any overarching theory of learning. Louise Stoll and Dean Fink's book on school improvement (1995) includes a list which helpfully fuses cognitive processes and emotional attitudes:

* abstraction – the capacity for discovering patterns and meanings

* systems thinking – to see relationships between phenomena

- experimentation – the ability to find one's own way through continuous learning

- the social skills to collaborate with others

- creative problem solving

- the use of advanced organizers

- graphic representations

- metacognition.

Perkins' *Smart schools* (1992), which builds upon the concept of distributed cognition to discover new ways of developing schools as places for learning, is complemented by Senge's *Schools that learn* (2000) with its emphasis on learning for school development. Stoll, Fink and Earl's *It's about learning – and it's about time* (2003) brings the two issues together.

In the USA, the large voluntary networks of Essential Schools, Accelerated Schools and so on are based around a striving for deeper learning. The New Basics project in Queensland seeks to align new models of curriculum, pedagogy and assessment; its twenty 'productive pedagogies' emphasise engaged and reflective learning.

Substantive conversation: In classes with substantive conversation there is considerable teacher-student and student-student interaction about the ideas of a substantive topic; the interaction is reciprocal, and it promotes coherent shared understanding. Features include:

(a) intellectual substance

(b) dialogue – the sharing of ideas which is not completedly scripted or controlled by one party

(c) logical extension and synthesis

(d) a sustained exchange.

(Education Queensland website)

Each of these *productive pedagogies* is presented through an explanation, a 'continuum of practice' which provides a means of auditing current practice, and a descriptive example. There is a social and moral coherence about this project, which simultaneously deals with cognitive and affective development, and seeks to promote a response to a rapidly changing world which is based on principles of social justice and citizenship.

In Europe, the concept of 'pedagogy' is central to school development. This has helped to avoid a divorce between School Improvement as a study of processes, school cultures and change management, and other fields of educational studies such as sociology, psychology and pedagogy. It is important to understand that in many European countries the concept of pedagogy means more than just teaching methods; it requires an articulation of educational aims and processes in social, ethical and affective as well as cognitive terms, and involves reflection about the changing nature of society or the value of human existence. This contrasts with Anglo-American conceptions of 'methodology' which have often been too linear, as in Tyler's content–teaching–assessment model:

Teaching and learning involves a more complex, dynamic and contradictory interplay between:

- curriculum as values as well as content
- inherited patterns of teaching, along with the individual teacher's personality and preferred styles
- the school ethos and environment, interacting with the culture of the wider society
- a general theory of learning, and individual learners' preferred learning styles.

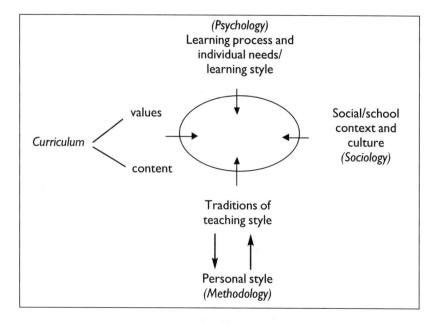

This model of pedagogy can be adapted to a range of different situations and texts, for example a newspaper editorial or a television programme. In these cases we often find an alignment between the different elements. In the popular television cookery series *The Naked Chef*, for example, Jamie Oliver's casual but fast-moving personal style combines with curricular values of openness and flexibility (not fussing about the finer details) to reach out to a postmodern audience with a constant desire to try out new things but not much spare time. The alignment is much harder to find in schools, where rigid time frames, authoritarian relationships and an over-tested content-heavy curriculum clash with adolescent lifestyles and youth culture. Attempts to transform learning based on new understandings of cognition are repeatedly undermined by existing school structures (the organisation of time, space, people and resources).

It is difficult to see how school improvement can move forward without analysing and recognising these contradictions. Further progress towards the 'learning organisation' and school development which is open to alternative futures requires a coherent rethinking of pedagogy.

CHAPTER EIGHT

Schools for citizens

> *By the year 2000 we should be number one in the world in the percentage
> of eighteen year olds that are politically and socially involved. Far more
> important than our mathematics and our science scores is the involvement
> of the next generation in maintaining our democracy and helping those
> within it that need assistance – the young, the ill, the old, the retarded,
> the illiterate, the hungry and the homeless. Schools that cannot turn out
> politically active and socially helpful citizens should be identified, and
> their rates of failure announced in the newspapers.*
>
> (David Berliner, 1993)

> *Citizenship implies freedom – to work, to eat, to dress, to wear shoes, to
> sleep in a house, to support onself and one's family, to love, to be angry, to
> cry, to protest . . . Citizenship is not obtained by chance: it is a construc-
> tion that, never finished, demands we fight for it.*
>
> (Paulo Freire 1998)

Education for Citizenship, a recent addition to the curriculum in Britain,
poses a creative challenge for school improvement. The intersection of
citizenship with pedagogy, curriculum, school ethos, the wider community, and school development processes, including possible conflicts of
values, makes it difficult to regard it as simply a discrete addition to the
curriculum. It has the potential, if taken seriously, to challenge current
trends in school development – if not a Trojan horse, it is at least a Trojan
mouse.

Teachers elsewhere are invariably surprised, not by its introduction but
that it was ever missing. In Germany for example, *politische Bildung*
(political education) has been an accepted part of the secondary school
curriculum for decades. No one appears to doubt its importance, as a
contribution to ensuring that no future generation will fall under the
influence of fascism. Similar democratic motives recur in other parts of
Europe, with their various histories.

While most countries have a version of education for citizenship, under a variety of titles, its political orientation can vary enormously.

> The movement for democracy in China and the demonstrations in Tiananmen Square were an inspiring moment. In particular, in the confrontation with the army, the picture of the student in front of the tanks throws up a vital problem relating to both democracy and citizenship: in essence, there are two models of citizen – the twenty year olds in the tank and the twenty year olds in front of the tank. (Henry Maitles 2001: 23)

In chapter 6, I used a 'three orientations' model of the curriculum:

- academic/vocational – based on the intention of adapting the young to a pre-existing social structure

- liberal-progressive – based on the premise that promoting empathy and individual sensibility would lead naturally to a better world

- socially-critical – enabling young people to question and challenge unjust social structures and values, including direct social engagement during the years of schooling rather than being deferred until adulthood. (Kemmis *et al* 1983)

Some versions of education for citizenship – often bearing the title Civics – are designed to promote conformity and obedience. The earlier but short-lived introduction of citizenship as a cross-curricular dimension in the National Curriculum for England and Wales in 1990 placed a heavy emphasis on 'duty, the importance of wealth creation, and the family' in line with the political preoccupations of the Thatcher government (Brown 2000: 114). The values of monarchy and Empire pervaded the school curriculum of late Victorian and early 20th century Britain through literature, history, geography and religious instruction.

Many approaches based on social awareness and empathy can best be described as liberal-progressive. Progressive teachers of English, in many English-speaking countries from the 1970s onwards, aimed to develop sensitivity, emotional development and human values by reading literature and performing drama, but this was limited by its disconnection from other subjects. Thus, the poems of Wilfred Owen and Siegfried Sassoon helped to make young people less naive about the glory of war, but they developed little sense of how the First World War had resulted from imperial rivalries, nor that collective popular action in Russia, Germany and elsewhere had been able to end it. Similarly, in geography lessons, children might develop a feeling for the fragility of the environment but have no opportunity of campaigning to protect it. The divisions between one subject and another, and between knowledge and action, cognition and emotion, school learning and the outside world, placed serious limitations on these embryonic forms of education for citizenship.

The new model of citizenship education has the potential to overcome these limitations and to develop into a socially-critical curriculum, though this is by no means guaranteed. The Crick Report provides a basis for more engaged and authentic forms of learning by identifying three complementary and interlocking strands:

* social and moral responsibility

* community involvement

* political literacy.

However, the direction of education for citizenship is inevitably sharply contested, including attempts by all kinds of agencies to rebrand their resources under its logo. There is even a resource pack available from the British Army. Students could conceivably help out in various community groups, under the rubric of 'active citizenship', but without the opportunity for evaluative discussion.

The success of Education for Citizenship depends upon substantial change at a whole-school level. It raises key issues for the School Improvement project, as it potentially challenges dominant practices and ideologies of schooling.

Learning and teaching

Education for citizenship cannot simply be seen as an add-on. We need to relate citizenship and personal and social development, within a human rights perspective, to core practices and beliefs across the curriculum. A separate set of lessons on citizenship is of little use if all the other lessons socialise towards passivity and blind obedience.

When Dickens characterised Mr Gradgrind's teaching as pouring facts into empty vessels, he was making a political as well as a methodological critique. In *Hard Times*, he pours scorn on schooling which shows no respect for the knowledge which children gain in their everyday lives, from their families and communities. Though much has changed in the past 150 years, the period in which Dickens was writing has had an enduring influence on schools up to the present day. Despite surface differences, his satire essentially represents a default model of teaching on which we tend to fall back whenever we stop thinking about alternatives.

Behaviourism now has little credibility as a general theory of learning, but implicitly underlies many didactic practices. It ostensibly presents a more scientific explanation than Dickens' metaphor, but it is reductionist; Pavlov's and Skinner's conditioning of caged animals provides an alarming metaphor for school learning, and an impoverished model of human learning in general. It can't even account for the learning of the proverbially curious cat. It is also inherently *undemocratic*. For behaviourists, learning is definitely something you do to children.

If children accept that 4×4 makes 16 simply for the reward, as behaviourists recommend, we are turning them into unquestioning victims, not citizens. What if we were to reward them for agreeing that the earth is really flat? Or, to use a more realistic example, for believing that Jews or maybe Palestinians are 'vermin' rather than fellow human beings?

The following characteristics of learning in too many classrooms are problematic, not only in terms of a psychology of learning but in their implications for citizenship.

(a) The teacher is the main source of information. (Sometimes information comes from a book or computer, but rarely from a child, parents or the outside world.)

(b) Knowledge appears as fragments of facts, with limited connections and little opportunity to evaluate its truth or moral implications.

(c) The learners are largely passive, their role being to absorb facts or to practise set moves before demonstrating their acquisition back to the teacher.

(d) Factual knowledge and the acquisition of motor skills predominate over evaluation or higher-level cognitive development, and are divorced from emotional and social development.

(e) The learning doesn't link with prior experience, and is divorced from the wider society or environment.

(f) Active cooperation in groups is rare and most time is spent either listening as a whole class or practising as an individual.

(g) There is no space for social action which will utilise or test out new knowledge and ideas.

Corson (1998: 100) points to the following authoritarian aspects of the standard teaching conventions which we simply take for granted, but which actively undermine self-esteem and students' rights on a daily basis in our schools:

- the unrestrained use of the imperative (by the teacher)
- the use of the (absolute) right to speak last
- the use of the (absolute) right to contradict
- the use of the (absolute) right to define the world for others
- the use of the (absolute) right to interrupt or to censure
- the use of the (absolute) right to praise or blame in public.

We see these practices directly undermining learning which ought to promote citizenship. In Scotland, which avoided the Thatcher Government's curriculum reform and its censorship of contemporary social studies, Modern Studies has equal status to history and geography, but to a considerable extent its respectability has been bought at the price of an 'academic' approach to knowledge. My own analysis of two recent and very popular textbooks for 15–17 year olds revealed the following characteristics:

(a) There is little acknowledgement of the student's personal experience (for example, in a passage about old people with dementia, or in a chapter about racism).

(b) Student tasks involve much memorisation and collection of data, and some low-level interpretation (e.g. of a graph), but little opportunity for evaluation, research or critical reading.

(c) Even seemingly realistic tasks ('Why are stereotypical viewpoints dangerous'; 'Prepare a short speech in which you explain why women are under-represented in Parliament') are presented as paper exercises for the teacher to mark, rather than opportunities to interact with a real audience.

(d) Virtually all tasks are intended for individuals, rather than as co-operative activities.

(e) There is almost no attempt to relate cognitive understanding to affective, or knowledge to action.

By contrast, Political Education in Germany emphasises engaged learning which is cooperative and related to action. Action is categorised as:

- real action (e.g. investigations, placements, asking local experts, street interviews)
- simulated action (e.g. role play, games, decision games, debates)

- production (i.e. as an outcome of learning, the students produce reports, a video, a newspaper or exhibition, or simply make a presentation to their class). (Herdegen 2001)

These practices are important not only for citizenship education but for school improvement more generally; they might provide a means to make learning more engaged, realistic and challenging, and create opportunities for personal and social development.

Curriculum

It comes as a shock to find Danish teachers advised not to overplan in advance, as this can undermine their negotiations with students about what to learn. The same document suggests that 14–16 year olds should themselves take the initiative of inviting speakers into school or arranging visits, rather than their teachers doing it. (Ministry of Education, Denmark 1995)

Teachers in Britain have become so accustomed to every detail of the curriculum being decided from above that the idea of negotiation sounds almost revolutionary. From an early age, children learn that they have no right to choose: the literacy hour has virtually removed all opportunities for individual choice of books to read; individual choice of topics for research has been squeezed out by the push to cover content. Literacy is predefined in terms of genres and linguistic terminology for every term of primary school, regardless of children's needs or interests. The increasing frequency of tests has tightened control for secondary students. Scottish 17-year-olds studying for the Higher have formal assessments almost every week; in Geography alone, they have to complete 14 different tests in two terms to be eligible for the examination, and no time for frivolities such as fieldwork! The AS-level in England means that Year 12 – once a time for encouraging deeper thinking and wider reading – is no longer free of examination pressure.

This regime is not conducive to citizenship. Adult society does need to set out what it feels is most important to pass on to the next generation, but young people in Britain now experience an imposition which far exceeds this necessity, and denies young people's rights. Who, for example, decreed that all 7–11 year olds would study Anglo-Saxon Britain, and why? That all children in the third term of Year 5 need to learn the meaning of personification? The selection of content is often arbitrary, and denies particular groups the right to see themselves represented in what counts as legitimate knowledge. In the words of the principal of a multiethnic school in downtown Toronto, 'Why should my students be learning about a barbaric medieval Europe – knights hitting each other over the head with lumps of metal, and disastrous levels of public hygiene – when the Islamic or Chinese civilisation at that time was far more advanced?' Clearly, we are dealing not with the simple imposition of curriculum by adults on children and adolescents but a powerful elite's claim to represent society as a whole.

There has to be a compromise between the adult world's responsibilities and the interests of the young. The Danish curriculum (see Chapter 6) suggests that a class might embark on a major topic either because students raise it, perhaps because of a recent event, or because the teacher raises the issue. In either case, discussion and interaction between teacher and students leads to a range of questions and problems which individuals and small groups in the class can then choose to pursue.

The time frame for study, its division into periods taught by too many separate subject specialists, often mitigates against deeper learning. In many parts of Germany, timetables are suspended for Project Week, so that students can work as a class on a major topic, or regroup with students from other classes. It is recommended that a planning group consisting of teachers and students display suggested themes beforehand, but that individuals can post suggestions too.

The relationship between citizenship and curriculum is not exhausted by questions of pupil choice and timetable. In Britain, we tend to fight shy of more controversial issues. Whereas British teachers tend to privilege middle of the road viewpoints, the emphasis in Germany, following the Beutelsbach Conference, is for teachers to be open about controversiality, present a wide range of views, and acknowledge their own standpoint.

Teaching about controversial issues: the Beutelsbach Consensus (Germany)

(1) You must not overpower. It is unethical to take pupils unawares, however that is done, in imposing preferred opinions, and thus to prevent learners reaching an independent judgement.

(2) Whatever is controversial in social science and in politics must also appear controversial in teaching.

(3) Pupils must be placed in a position where they can analyse a political situation and their own interests and position, and also to look for ways and means of influencing the social situation they find themselves in.

(Hans-Georg Wehling: Konsens à la Beutelsbach? Nachlese zu einem Expertengespräch. In S. Schiele, H. Schneider, eds, p. 179)

Teachers have a responsibility to evaluate standard practices carefully, including those which are apparently progressive. Circle time in primary schools has created new opportunities for discussion, but can be subverted into a disciplinary function, or even an opportunity to correct speech habits (see Claire 2001: 154).

School ethos and human rights

In rethinking school organisation and ethos, we need to ask political questions about educational purpose, and what we mean by a good school. Ethos cannot simply be seen, instrumentally, as a means of improving exam results, although it is crucial in doing so. We need to relate the quality of school life and relationships to the human rights of young people during the years of schooling. This is particularly true in schools serving disadvantaged communities; in successful inner-city schools, the daily experiences of schooling reaffirm a sense of human dignity, rather than appearing to confirm a lack of status and value.

This is why 'orderly behaviour', as a key characteristic of effective schools, is so misleading. Schools which appear orderly on the surface can have a negative and combative culture. Charlotte Carter's action research project in a boys' comprehensive school in the English West Midlands revealed a culture in which hostility and disparagement had become the norm, and were profoundly affecting self-esteem and achievement.

> The school just expects us to do wrong and that's the way we get to be involved in what happens . . . They seem to think we are totally selfish and want to wreck the school.

> Your mates are always knocking you . . . it's easier just to see things the way they do and then you don't get disappointed. Say you miss a goal, you still know you are okay really, but the rest of the team might force you to feel bad and then you do.

Charlotte Carter offers the following interpretation:

> The participants' self-image was tentative and precariously dependent on their daily negotiation of conflicting information about who they wanted to be and what they were told they were. As a result they were held back by a quagmire of self-doubt and by dependence on others and the school, neither of which was felt to be safe or just. (Carter 2000: 155)

There is increasing understanding that it is better to involve students in establishing codes of behaviour. Rules imposed from above will always be resisted and are never fully internalised. 'We'll always cause problems because we don't like adults ordering us to do things . . . A rule is a convention if you've made it your own . . . it's inside us' (Alderson 2000: 127).

There are signs that some schools are moving to a conscious understanding of ethos change in terms of democracy and human rights. The work of the Scottish School Ethos Network has been important in developing this perspective, and its case study reports are encouraging (www.ethos-net.co.uk). The democratic involvement of pupils takes time, but releases initiative which can also ultimately reduce the pressure on teachers and heads.

Encouraging pupils to take more responsibility is hard work, but can also reduce anxiety. We had local politicians visiting, and I suddenly realised that I hadn't noticed it was raining and we needed games and activities out for breaktime. I needn't have worried: some older children had organised it themselves for Primary 1 and 2 – they'd spontaneously taken on the responsibility.

At the School Council, pupils suggested restarting the Bullying Advice Centre (run by pupils). The next week, I felt very guilty that I hadn't done anything about this. The pupils said, 'Mrs Howarth, we know you've been very busy. We put the notices up, and it's already running'.

Carol Howarth, Headteacher, Spittal Primary School, Glasgow (*Improving Schools* 4/1)

'I've decided to cancel the Pay-to-Park event. You are not well enough organised, you haven't done the publicity . . . I don't have time between now and next week . . .'

I was surprised then, the following Friday, to arrive at the school gates (in my car) to a large group of pupils with collection buckets and a huge banner. In my absence they had gone ahead on their own.

What struck me most was that they were genuinely in control, empowered. They became 'co-creators and participants in the evolution of the school' (Senge).

Michael Farrell, Portobello High School, Edinburgh (*Improving Schools* 5/2)

Community involvement

Traditionally, our schools have been oriented more towards competitive individualism than supportive cooperation. This has implications both for achievement and for citizenship. The inclusion of community involvement as a strand within education for citizenship has a trans-formative potential for education generally. We tend to take for granted the limited opportunities for learning beyond the school gate, regarding it as a major victory if geography students take part in a field trip every year or two, 15 year olds have a week's work experience before they leave school, or primary school children occasionally go out into the country-side. Some schools do better than this, but they are the exception.

Visits and placements provide highly motivating sources of learning. Rushey Mead School, Leicester, has for some years devoted one after-noon a week for its senior pupils to a combined citizenship and PSE pro-gramme which includes placements in community groups (Wrigley 2000: 55). Students who helped to redecorate a women's refuge, for example, brought back to school an important awareness which could not have been gained from a lecture. Community placements potentially change the balance between teachers and learners, making the learning relationship more reciprocal and symmetrical. Some schools in the USA are beginning to explore an 'apprenticeship' model of learning by arrang-ing extended work-placements. This enables inner-city youngsters to experience careers which they would otherwise think unattainable. We should not forget the importance, however, of ensuring that the practical experiences are complemented by the opportunity to question, discuss and critically evaluate the practices which are observed.

It is too easy to underestimate the life experience of inner-city children. Citizenship education, like PSE, is in danger of skimming the surface and having little real impact unless we find ways of engaging even disturbing experiences. Hilary Claire, in an illuminating book about children in two London primary schools, provides many examples. She demonstrates how young children are not only suffering the direct effects of poverty, but also feel the disparagement by others of their condition. Some use poverty to stigmatise and abuse each other.

> I get in lots of fights. Sometimes people force you, get you mad, you try and ignore, but you can't . . . they say about your family, you can't afford to get a house . . . most of the time it's about your family. They call you . . . you're a pig, and your mum doesn't even wear proper clothes, you can't afford to buy things . . . If you walk down the street and you see this drunk man, or tramp, they'll go: that's your father. That tramp looks just like you, the clothes you're wearing. (Claire 2001: 36).

She suggests that children need the opportunity of circle time for sharing and discussing experience, but that other less public interactions are needed so that children can be sufficiently open with trusted adults about the difficulties in their lives.

Unless we learn to connect with the experience of poverty, our school improvement efforts will fail to engage creatively with the challenge of raising achievement. The general message so far from official channels has been to reinforce the boundaries between school and community in the interests of minimising distractions to school learning.

Personal identity, power and school development

It is a serious contradiction in New Labour policies for education that teachers without rights are expected to explain them to children. The low-trust high-surveillance culture referred to in Chapter 3 cuts across the rhetoric of human rights which teachers are being asked to introduce into schools, and hinders the initiative and creativity which they will need to bring about necessary transformation. Teachers will need to assert their own citizenship in order to share it.

The further development of curriculum and pedagogy, in an age of such dramatic change, requires commitment, cooperation and imagination. It involves the engagement of teachers with theory and with the transformation of everyday practice.

Recent developments in learning theory around the idea of situated cognition, initially conceived in terms of work-based learning, need to be extended into the humanities. A particularly interesting feature of lessons observed in some multiethnic schools (Wrigley 2000; also 2000a) was the use of creative arts techniques such as imaginative writing and drama to explore aspects of belief and cultural practice. In one lesson, girls studying *Romeo and Juliet* improvised a scene that Shakespeare did not write – an encounter between the three main women: Juliet, her mother and her nurse, after her father has commanded her to marry the man of his choice. In a religious education lesson, pupils wrote their personal Creeds, in which they characteristically moved from orthodox religious faith to a formulation of personal belief.

Visual arts and music were also used to explore questions of personal and cultural identity. In other lessons, a study of the semiotics of journalism and television drama led to a deeper understanding of the ideological functioning of everyday texts.

I believe in one God but he does not control us.

Instead he guides everyone towards the right things.

I believe in Evolution. It does happen

but very slowly so we do not even notice it.

I believe that everyone is equal

No man is higher or lower than anyone else.

(Wrigley 2000: 69)

These forms of 'border pedagogy', to borrow Henry Giroux's phrase, all took place among bilingual pupils of South Asian heritage. For many, they provided a means of re-evaluating their complex cultural heritage and re-positioning themselves for the future. Without such opportunities, children and adolescents may find it difficult to reconcile family cultures and beliefs with the lifestyles of contemporary Western society. It is essential to do this in an open-ended way, in order to avoid the prejudice that modern Western ways are superior, and the creative arts provide an important means to do so.

This question is equally important, however, for monolingual students. They too need to develop a critical consciousness of the dominant ideologies which surround them and which ordinarily they simply take for granted. As the anthropologist Margaret Mead once said, the fish is the last creature to discover water. In this era of globalisation, consumerism, militarism and the assumption of Western superiority are a form of fundamentalism as powerful as any religion. The creative arts and semiotic studies such as literature and the media encourage an emotional as well as an intellectual response and provide a medium for learning and development which engages young people actively and critically.

CHAPTER NINE

Communities of learning

It takes a whole village to raise a child.
(African proverb)

We take too much for granted the strong boundary between schools and the wider world. This has deep roots in history. The monastic schools of the Middle Ages offered learning to some village children at the price of isolation from the world and its wickedness. Given the mission of Victorian public education to domesticate the unruly offspring of the industrial working class, parents tended to be seen as the enemy rather than as potential collaborators. Only the church minister and an occasional wealthy benefactor were allowed through the door.

The boundary has weakened in recent decades, but the walls remain high and often unscalable. Parents of young children, once kept securely outside, are now encouraged to come inside the school at the start and end of the day, and often to help in the classroom. However, parents may experience resistance when their views, including their knowledge of their own children, contradict a teacher's assumptions. The possibility for liaison and influence is also differentiated by class and race. Meanwhile little has changed in secondary schools, and community schools, despite their proven value, remain the exception. The school improvement literature has emphasised the importance of parents, but in a one-sided way. In official advice, the parents' role is primarily to ensure that children attend school and do their homework.

At the same time, we have tended to take for granted the internal organisation of schools, and failed to question whether they offer a quality experience of community life. It has become unfashionable to devote attention to restructuring, and the extent to which structure constrains and determines culture needs re-emphasis.

In this chapter, I wish to argue the importance of both these aspects of community for school improvement, namely:

• how schools, and particularly larger secondary schools, function as communities for young people

• how schools relate to a wider community life beyond their doors.

The problem of the large school

Loss of community is a concern for many urban societies, and deeply affects the climate for school learning. Unfortunately, rather than providing a means for community building, many larger secondary schools tend to replicate and reinforce the problems of the wider society.

Sergiovanni (1999: 9 seq.) reminds us of Tönnies' distinction between *Gesellschaft* and *Gemeinschaft* (normally translated as society and community, though the German implies an opposition between merely living *alongside* one another and sharing a *common life*). *Gesellschaft* involves encounters which are transactional and impersonal, in which meaning and significance are often difficult to find. People strive for their own advantage, and manage to coexist through politeness. Subjectivity is frowned upon and rationality prized. Sergiovanni argues that these are also prime characteristics of many schools.

Often, and especially where there is family breakdown and in the absence of extended family structures, adolescents seek community elsewhere, such as on the street. Sergiovanni argues that schools need to provide an alternative to teenage gangs by developing a strong and meaningful community life. We need to remember the African proverb: it takes a whole village to raise a child. It cannot be done by individual teachers working in isolation from each other, each in their own box and slice of time.

A real community is inherently educational. Its values and knowledge are taught to new members and celebrated in customs and rituals. 'Community of kinship, place and mind, in time becomes a community of memory.' (*ibid*: 8) Sergiovanni argues for new school structures as a framework for the development of nurturing communities:

> We have lost vital parts of a good education: the neighbourhood and family. While we cannot return to a simpler time, we must still find ways to give children a secure place to grow up, an opportunity to play and create a chance to converse with adults. (*ibid*: 11)

Until the 1960s, under a selective school system, most secondary schools in Britain had fewer than 500 students. A key criterion in determining the size of the new comprehensive schools was the need to have a sufficiently large cohort entering at age 11 or 12 to sustain a final stage which could offer a wide range of subject choice, matched to different types of interest or ability. Little attention was given to the impact on younger adolescents of entering a school of a thousand or more students.

Various attempts were made to provide a sense of belonging, through a pastoral system based on houses or year groups. This was a pallid imitation of the house system of the independent boarding schools – residential communities held together symbolically by participation in competitive sports and cultural activities. Meeting briefly as a registration class once a day provides an inadequate anchor point to generate a sense of belonging. In Scotland, the pastoral care system was professionalised through the designation of carefully chosen staff as Guidance Teachers, who were given responsibility for teaching Personal and Social Education and released from a significant amount of subject teaching, but this has had the drawback of allowing others to become simply subject specialists without a broader responsibility.

Despite attempts to remedy the situation through these pastoral structures, the basic problems of size and anonymity remain. In most British secondary schools, subject teachers are allocated to younger classes on a random basis, such that twelve to fifteen people teaching a class of twelve year olds have no further contact with each other – hardly a good basis for teamwork and collective planning. Geography or music teachers, with limited curriculum time, might teach hundreds of different children a week. Research by Maurice Galton and others (see Croll 1983: 82) on transition to secondary school shows that children make far less progress in their first year at secondary school than previously, and around a third actually regress. Another member of this research team Sara Delamont (1983) demonstrates how the specialist teacher system cultures pupils into far greater dependency than at primary school. Especially in more troubled neighbourhoods, pastoral/guidance teams make phenomenal efforts to repair the damage of children's sense of alienation, but the system itself is dysfunctional and can exacerbate distressed and distressing behaviour.

The situation is not dissimilar in other countries with large urban populations, but solutions are being found. One answer is to divide large schools into smaller units, such as the halls of Stantonbury Campus in England. In this highly successful school, each hall is allocated a team of teachers with responsibility for most of their subjects. The team has a degree of autonomy in planning the use of time and people, cooperates

144 SCHOOLS OF HOPE

together in teaching and curriculum planning, and assumes responsibility for guidance and parental liaison.

A different pattern has been established for 11–12 year olds at Falinge Park School, Rochdale, where each class has a single teacher for over 40 per cent of the timetable. The class teacher is responsible for English, humanities subjects, and Personal and Social Education. Teachers receive support from other members of the team if they lack experience in a particular subject. The system provides emotional stability at a critical time of school transition. The teachers are able to relate to each individual and respond to different learning needs and preferred learning styles. For the rest of the timetable, the number of teachers is strictly limited, including a carousel system for creative arts, and the class teacher is able to act as an effective anchor point. Inspectors were impressed by this system, and concluded that children were making much faster progress on average than is normal, without the usual regression of the transition year. The school was soon nominated to be a Beacon School (Wrigley 2000: 91).

In Germany, a number of large comprehensive schools have implemented the small-group-model (Team-Kleingruppen-Modell – see Sergiovanni 1999; Ratzki 1996). In this system, not only is there a 'mini-school' consisting of about five classes and eight teachers, but the students work for much of their time within smaller mixed-ability groups. The group members learn to cooperate together and engage in tasks which develop their academic and social responsibility.

Teachers in Denmark are qualified in three different subjects and most students up to the age of 16 have no more than four or five different teachers each year. The main class teacher normally stays with the class for more than one year. This creates the basis for more democratic forms of learning in which there is greater flexibility and choice for the learner, and in which the cognitive and social needs of a full range of learners can be met.

In Norway, 13–16 year olds enjoy a similar system. Teachers do not belong to subject departments but to year teams, so that a team of five teachers is able to cover the whole curriculum. Teachers do not teach the children in other years unless they need to fill up their timetables. This arrangement makes it unnecessary to have parallel teams of guidance or support staff, or extended management systems.

The Coalition of Essential Schools in the United States works on the principle that no teacher should teach more than 80 students altogether. Although each school differs in its internal organisation, it is generally felt that promoting deeper learning requires a more extended contact between each teacher and a class (www.essentialschools.org).

These structures are different, but they are all designed to enable teachers to:

- work successfully with mixed ability classes

- negotiate appropriate work to match the various interests and abilities

- integrate learners with special needs

- relate well with their students

- create a sense of security and care

- support the social development of the class

- and promote more engaged and active learning.

Teams of teachers working in co-operation, and the improved social climate and relationships in a reasonably small learning community, would make it possible for many schools to reduce class size, since there would be less need for separate pastoral, managerial or learning support staff. This would make far better use of the overall 17:1 pupil: teacher ratios in the average British secondary school than the present elaborate structures which result in many classes of 30 pupils.

Community schools

The term 'community school' covers a wide variety of organisations, and many schools function as community schools even without the formal designation and funding. Though some individual schools are described in the school improvement literature, the concept as a whole has not been adequately explored, nor the impact of community schooling on ethos and achievement.

Basing some adult education classes in a school building may be a starting point, but it would be a mistake to confuse this minimalist position (sometimes adopted simply for reasons of economy) with genuine community education. There is no single pattern, but the common motive is to secure mutual benefit from the participation of young people and adults. School students might help in a nursery so that young mothers are able to attend qualification courses. Other students might interview senior citizens attending a social club in the school building. Community schools have the potential to be more than an economic amalgamation of different kinds of provision; there should be an impact on the curriculum.

There is no masterplan, and each school finds its own way forward; leadership means building on previous success. Thomas Hepburn School, Gateshead, established an electronic link with schools in Norway, France and Italy. As part of a multinational history project, the pupils accompanied older people attending their social centre to Beamish open air museum. They gained in confidence and communication skills, checking the museum's view of history against the older people's narratives. Their information was then exchanged internationally using internet and email.

Community schools help to bring parents into contact with teachers. In particular, the widespread interest in computer skills has created an opportunity to rethink student–teacher and child–parent roles. In the *Family e-Learning* programme at Monkseaton, near Newcastle, 17-year-old students work as technicians and tutors to provide computer skills classes for whole families. Children at Seymour Park Primary School (Trafford, Manchester) run courses for their parents, as well as staff development courses for their teachers (Wrigley 2000).

> The children are now running training sessions for their teachers and for parents. We help the children to be good teachers, by asking them to plan carefully and consider what the adults will most need to know, and where their difficulties may lie, exactly duplicating the process which an adult teacher might use.
>
> There was a wonderful moment last year when a Sikh boy taught his grandfather how to use the internet and access photographs of Indian cities he hadn't visited since he was a child. Word of this spread fast, and we are now seeking funding for a community ICT room, which we hope will evolve into a full-blown community learning centre.
>
> (Jenny Dunn, Headteacher, Seymour Park School, in Wrigley 2000: 38)

Other schools working in depressed areas help to provide parents with qualifications. At Sparrow Hill School, Rochdale, mothers of Pakistani origin attend courses provided at their request by the local College, though they would find it difficult to travel alone to the College's main campus. Their sense of achievement is motivating not only for themselves but for their children; it has helped to enhance a respect for learning (Wrigley 2000: 145).

Community schools can work to empower marginalised groups through community development projects in which informal learning is linked to the generation of new democratic structures. Freire's practices and

philosophy have been adapted by community educators in more industrial countries such as Britain. Community development projects can
also directly involve young people in schools. In some schools in
Northumberland, England, youth workers helped students develop concrete plans for improving their area. A development grant had already
been earmarked, so that the young people would learn positive lessons
from their involvement, rather than risk frustration if good ideas failed to
materialise.

The New Community School (see website) is a model being piloted
across Scotland, based on the North American 'full service school'.
Various service agencies are brought together around a school or cluster
of schools, such as adult education, social services, health education and
housing. Within this general model, local schools and communities are
free to develop their own structures and priorities.

Parents as partners

Just when parents were taking a greater role and interest in their
children's education, the 1988 Education Reform Act in England and
Wales reconstructed their role as *consumers* within a system of market
choice. (The reality of school choice depends, of course, upon parents
having sufficient material resources and cultural capital to get their
children into the 'best' schools; for many, consumer choice is like window
shopping with an empty purse.)

Positioning parents as consumers gives some a temporary influence at the
point of enrolment, but little positive influence during the years their
children spend at a school. Despite tokenistic steps to establish more
direct channels of influence, such as the election of a few parents to the
governing body and an annual parents' meeting, parental involvement is
slight compared with many parts of Northern Europe; even the governing bodies have limited room for manoeuvre given centralised control of
the agenda for change.

Much of the legislative change assumes a one-way relationship between
schools and parents. The school's statutory responsibility to report on
a child's attainment supports the consumer relationship, but not an
active partnership in supporting learning. Both sides can feel threatened:
teachers become suspicious of parents, who appear to take on the role of
watchdogs, while the parents of non-attenders are threatened with with-
drawal of welfare benefits and even imprisonment. This is hardly a basis
on which to establish a trusting partnership. By comparison, good practice in many parts of Scandinavia assumes a termly meeting between the

class teacher and parents at which curriculum content and methods are openly discussed.

The introduction of home-school contracts further reinforces the sense that education is something that only schools can do, with parents relegated to a supportive or even a custodial role. True partnership cannot be achieved through such a bureaucratic device.

> Knowing what we know about the importance of parents listening to and reading with their children does not justify putting pressure on parents to sign a home-school agreement in which they commit themselves to spending set periods on such activities.
>
> Where there is already confidence and trust between home and school and between individual teachers and families, such schemes will already be in place . . . Where such trust is lacking or where parents and teachers do not value one another, contractual agreements are worthless. (Mittler 2000: 157)

Fortunately, there are more positive and imaginative forms of partnership-building in schools, and particularly with marginalised communities where barriers to communication are most entrenched. There is substantial evidence of the success of reading partnerships, where children take home books to read with their parents, along with a diary for comments. This provides a context for relaxed discussions with individual parents at the end of the school day. Teachers at Spittal Primary School, Glasgow, visit parents before their children join the school, but write first to emphasise the parents' right to turn down the offer of a visit if they wish. Many other schools now employ home-school liaison workers, often chosen from the local community (Wrigley 2001a).

There is strong evidence of the benefits of an active parental contribution. A study of young people who had escaped from disadvantage shows dramatic correlation between parental involvement and educational success (Pilling 1990: 196–7 in Mittler). This involved educationally stimulating activities, an explicit interest in learning, an emphasis on the importance of school work, and a sense of ambition for the child.

The barriers of prejudice

It is tempting, but extremely damaging, for teachers to assume that working-class or ethnic minority parents are uninterested in their children's education. Judgements are often made based on poor attendance at report evenings, without taking account of linguistic or cultural barriers, feelings of anxiety or inadequacy, or some parents' bad memories of their own school experience. Research such as the NFER survey (Jowett and Baginsky 1991) or Topping (1986) shows that parents living in areas of poverty and disadvantage are just as keen to help their children to learn (cited Mittler 2000: 156). Similar evidence elsewhere includes the Head Start programme in the United States (Sylva 1999).

The role of home-liaison teachers/assistants includes that of cultural mediation, in order to facilitate the partnership between school and parents, and overcome cultural misunderstandings.

The home-school liaison teacher at Whetley Park Primary School, Bradford, has many roles, including

• translating letters home

• interpreting at parents' nights

• explaining school procedures and expectations for newcomers

• acting as a mediator on issues of religious or cultural sensitivity

• helping parents understand the school's teaching methods

• showing parents how they can help their children's education at home.

The school invites parents to see what happens in classrooms, to see how teachers teach and what sort of work the children do. It also shows parents how household routines such as cooking can provide educational opportunities for language and maths. Parents are encouraged to teach pupils at home in the family language. They are encouraged to share books, talking with children about the pictures if their own reading in English is insufficient and asking older brothers and sisters to help.

As the home-school liaison teacher explained:

> This is a good staff. They are sensitive to parents and the culture. Parents don't come with suspicious feelings. They are keen to co-operate. They are very keen on education, even if sometimes they don't understand what we're doing. They've missed opportunities themselves, and will do anything to educate their children . . .
>
> There is a lot of co-operation, learning from each other's cultures. If we listen, then matters can be resolved. Some parents were against their children changing for PE, for religious reasons of modesty. They wanted the children to wear their normal clothes. The teachers felt loosely-fitting clothes made it difficult to see the children's movements. We reached a compromise by adopting tracksuits. (Wrigley 2000: 116)

Particular tensions surround links with parents of children identified as having special educational needs. Mittler stresses the importance of

> ridding oneself of any preconceptions about families, whether they are families who live in a particular area, have a child whose behaviour is particularly challenging or families who have already been labelled by others as 'difficult', 'rejecting' 'over-protective' or 'not yet come to terms with their child's difficulties', to give just a few examples of the most popular labels. (Mittler 2000: 159)

The rights of parents are now encoded in law, reflecting increasing recognition of the value of the parents' perspective, but this advice from a group of parents may serve to remind us of the distance still to be travelled.

- Please accept and value our children (and ourselves as families) as we are.

- Please celebrate difference.

- Please try and accept our children as children first. Don't attach labels to them unless you mean to do something.

- Please recognise your power over our lives. We live with the consequences of your opinions and decisions.

- Please understand the stress many families are under. The cancelled appointment, the waiting list no one gets to the top of, all the discussions about resources – it's our lives you're talking about.

- Don't put fashionable fads and treatments on to us unless you are going to be around to see them through. And don't forget families have many members, many responsibilities. Sometimes we can't please everyone.

- Do recognise that sometimes we are right! Please believe us and listen to what we know that we and our child need.

- Sometimes we are sad, tired and depressed. Please value us as caring and committed families and try to go on working with us.

(Russell 1997: 79, in Mittler 2000: 170)

A community perspective on learning

There is a deep gulf, in many different parts of the world, between school learning and the life of the host community. It is easy for teachers to overlook the knowledge and skills of the community, and unwittingly to convey a sense of arrogance. The extent of this problem was brought home to me by a teacher-educator from Papua New Guinea. Under the new curriculum there, teachers give agriculture lessons in schools. Unfortunately many have been disconnected, through their formal education, from sources of traditional knowledge and teach pupils to burn excess foliage rather than the indigenous method of recycling it back into the ground.

Some parents' knowledge is more acceptable to schools than others'. Sonia Nieto asks why American teachers regard skiing holidays in Europe as culturally enriching, but not travelling to Haiti to visit family (1999: 8). She argues that 'teachers need to build upon what [cultural capital] children do have, rather than lament about what they do not have'. Recalling her own childhood, she comments that there were few books, but reading the Sunday newspaper was a shared family activity, and many hours were spent around the kitchen table listening to family stories and folk tales.

We underestimate the knowledge and culture within working-class communities. The street of terraced houses where I grew up ('two up, two downs' with outside lavatories and no bathrooms) provided invaluable educational opportunities. I learned to play chess on the doorstep from an old man living three doors away. I was entranced by the power of Italian opera while I was still learning to read. (My uncle, who had left school at 14 and joined the navy during the Second World War, brought back from Italy recordings of the famous tenors Caruso and Gigli.) The corner grocer was a prime source of help with school projects: I remember him producing miniature packs of different varieties of tea and showing me where each had come from on a map of Asia. At the age of ten, I was keen to start learning foreign languages in secondary school – the Swiss mental health nurse who had moved in next door was multilingual. It came as a surprise, when qualifying to teach, to learn from a sociology lecture that I was *culturally deprived*!

Conditions change, and children growing up today on many housing schemes suffer a degree of poverty and cultural breakdown which would have been unimaginable in Britain in the 1960s. The problem remains, however, that schools know far too little about the knowledge, skills and culture embedded in the communities they serve, and community education services are too poorly resourced to develop it. In particular, council estates are thought of, in an undifferentiated way, as cultural deserts, if not concrete jungles. Ethnic minority communities fare better, but their cultures are often received by schools second-hand and in a tokenistic manner. It is almost unheard of for schools to draw upon the vast experiences of these communities, for example by inviting parents in to speak to classes about their travels, hobbies or jobs. Teachers of bilingual children are naturally anxious about them missing school during extended visits to relatives, but we rarely see attempts to draw on that experience educationally. This inevitably gives children the feeling that worthwhile knowledge comes from teachers, and that their own families and communities must be deeply ignorant. In order to be successful in school, they feel the need to reject family and community – a price that few are prepared to pay.

The development of community perspectives on learning provides a means for school improvement to combine a greater sense of social context with new pedagogical understandings. The recent work of Lave, Engeström and others (e.g. Lave and Wenger 1991; Engeström and Middleton 1996) provides models of cooperative and situated learning which may help overcome the tendency of schools to focus upon individualised learning, and help them relate to the more communal forms of learning within the community.

The inability of School Improvement theory so far to make a significant difference to schools in areas of poverty or ethnic difference points to a need to learn from community models rather than building higher walls round the school tradition through a pursuit of efficiency. We would do well to explore the concept of *learning community* in a more grounded sense, involving what happens outside the walls of the school and as well as within. Untold benefit could arise from a closer relationship between the fields of school improvement and community education.

CHAPTER TEN

Social justice – or a discourse of deficit?

> *What excellence is this that manages to coexist with more than a billion inhabitants of the developing world who live in poverty, not to say misery? Not to mention the all but indifference with which it coexists with 'pockets of poverty' and misery in its own, developed body*
>
> (Paulo Freire 1994)

It is a deep mistake to regard the dimension of social justice as an optional extra. Social divisions affect every aspect of school life and achievement, and do not disappear when we try to ignore them.

In Britain and elsewhere, an earlier emphasis on Equal Opportunities has suffered a partial eclipse through a new emphasis on Standards and Improvement. In the era of neo-liberalism, an understanding of the connections between underachievement and inequalities (gender, race, class, disability etc.) has been reframed into the vaguely moral demand to 'raise expectations'.

Accountability has been articulated in terms of raising average levels of attainment, rather than working for the broadest possible achievement and development of each individual. As a consequence, those to whom it is more difficult to 'add value' are construed as the problem, and only superficial attempts are made to accelerate progress.

Much of this book can be read as a response to that scenario. In fact, the concern for social justice runs through every chapter:

(1) an awareness of how the Effectiveness discourse focuses blame on individual schools for the consequences of poverty

(2) an exploration of the antidemocratic consequences of a dominant model of Improvement

(3) a surveillance regime which limits teachers' ability to respond personally to pupils, and acts as a career deterrent against teaching in inner-city schools

(4) the discriminatory effects of selective school systems and the quasi-market

(5) the importance of overcoming constructs of ability which lower expectations and restrict opportunities

(6) suggesting alternatives to a centrally controlled curriculum which does little to motivate young people and hinders them from understanding poverty and racism

(7) the need to replace teaching methods which silence and disempower the young

(8) the possibility of developing modes of learning which respect and promote human rights

(9) the need to establish rich partnerships between schools and communities, and to build learning communities on a human scale.

This chapter complements the preceding analyses by focusing in turn on various aspects of inequality (poverty; special educational needs; school exclusions; bilingualism; gender; racism and refugees). It seeks to reconnect them to a desire for school improvement, through a critique of the limitations of poorly theorised instrumentalist fixes and by suggesting more sustainable responses. The chapter is inevitably limited in its choice of sources and examples, and cannot hope to do justice to a rich professional literature in each of these areas.

While recognising the importance of specificity in analysis and response, there is an attempt to develop a more general theory by challenging discourses of deficit. Though some children inevitably seem harder to teach than others, the difficulty can be located in either the individual or in the intersection between learners and the school environment. The latter approach prefers to speak of 'barriers to learning' rather than individual disabilities and needs. It searches for solutions in terms of transforming the school environment and curriculum rather than in the forced assimilation of the child.

Within a discourse of deficit, many students are labelled as problems or even failures. The learning difficulties are essentialised and located within individuals. Those who cannot be assimilated or disciplined into 'normality' are segregated and excluded.

On a wider scale, however, there has been a strange twist to this pattern. In the English education system, entire schools with large numbers of 'problem children' have been officially declared failing, and their teachers scapegoated for the consequences of inexcusable levels of poverty. A discourse of deficit for pupils has been compounded by a discourse of derision for their teachers (see Ball 1990).

School Improvement has to move beyond a generalised and apolitical stance on high expectations, and get to grips with the research literature dealing with specific forms of inequality. It is crucial for school leaders to build alliances within and beyond the school, and to transform the structures and cultures which are obstacles to higher achievement for large numbers of pupils.

Facing up to poverty

Within a global trend of increasing poverty and social division, poverty in Britain (as in the USA) has dramatically increased in the last quarter century:

- 12,000,000 people (nearly a quarter of the population) are living in poverty in the UK – three times as many as in 1979

- From 1979 to 1993, the proportion of children living in households with incomes less than half the national average rose from 8 per cent to 32 per cent

- Over three-quarters of the 3,000,000 children living with only one parent are growing up in poverty (National Children's Home factfile 2000).

The links between poverty and low achievement are well established. In Britain, seven-year-olds from social class V (unskilled manual workers) are five times as likely to have reading difficulties as those from social class I (higher professions). By the age of 11, children with fathers in non-manual occupations are three years ahead in maths and reading, compared with children in social class V. Half the pupils entitled to free school meals have GCSE scores below 15 points, compared with one-sixth of those not on free school meals (National Child Development Study – summary in Mittler 2000: 52).

The Dearing Inquiry concluded that the doubling of university student numbers over a 20 year period had little impact on the proportion of students from lower socio-economic backgrounds. Recent data shows that nearly four out of five university places go to teenagers from non-manual backgrounds, and under 2 per cent from social class V (Plummer

2000: 38–9). The difficulties for students from lower-income families have been exacerbated by the abolition of grants and the levying of tuition fees, leading to high dropout rates.

Official data shows clearly that the attainment gap grows as children proceed through school. At 11, there is a substantial overlap (around 50 per cent) between higher attaining schools in the poorest areas and lower attaining schools in more affluent ones. By age 16, there is virtually none (DfES *Autumn Package*). A recent Inspectorate report *Improving City Schools* (Ofsted 2000), shows that, of the secondary schools with over 35 per cent of children on free meals, only 2 per cent even reach the national average.

It is clear that any effort to improve schools without dramatically reducing child poverty is like running up a downward escalator. A professional struggle to raise achievement necessarily also requires a political struggle for a more equal society.

Stephen Ball (1990) put a finger on the 'discourse of derision' by which policy makers seek to blame inferior working-class achievement on poor teaching and school leadership. The politicians rightly claim that 'the poor deserve better', but by stigmatising inner-city schools as failures, they generate a feeling that the communities themselves are failing. Conversely, successful school improvement serves to uplift a community, especially when the school is seen to be genuinely concerned about economic and social regeneration. An important step in 'turning round' a struggling school is to help the staff turn round to face up to poverty and engage with the life of the local community. (See also Hargreaves and Fullan 1998, although their expression 'move toward the danger' is altogether too negative.)

Establishing a positive image for a school, including changing its appearance and generating good publicity, is often thought of as a simple marketing exercise. In deprived working-class areas it may be more than this: people who have lost faith in their own abilities and self-worth may project their low expectations and lack of self-esteem onto the local school. A change of image helps to restore their hopes. School leaders need to develop a political understanding of their role, not only in the sense of relating to people and agencies locally, but also in terms of better understanding their place within the wider economic and political framework.

A typical curricular response to poverty is a reduction to 'the basics', a watered-down gruel of decontextualised literacy and numeracy exercises. The mainstream Effectiveness literature, based on an extremely narrow database, insists that this is the way to raise attainment. In the United States, federal funding for the poorest areas has diverted learners into a curriculum designed as remedial but which actually undermines motivation and becomes a trap. By contrast, the Accelerated Schools movement seeks to provide a meaningful challenge (see website). One of the few large-scale studies of curriculum enrichment in disadvantaged areas shows the importance of a challenging and meaningful curriculum which connects to students' experiences (Knapp 1995).

In the United States as in Britain, high-stakes testing is restricting learning opportunities by hindering teachers' attempts to develop meaningful curricula which will motivate disadvantaged young people.

> Teachers' creativity is diminished when they have to 'teach to the test' and are discouraged from implementing more engaging pedagogical practices. Darling-Hammond (1991) found a decline in the use of teaching and learning methods such as student-centered discussions, essay writing, research projects and laboratory work when standardized tests were required. (Nieto 1998: 422)

Skills remediation can best work when conducted on an intensive basis over short periods of time, and never as a long-term substitute for breadth, challenge and relevance.

Children whose different talents are developing at different speeds need experiences which will boost their confidence and give them a taste of success – rather than seeing themselves labelled as comparative failures in the three Rs. (Tim Brighouse 2002)

Despite the recent emphasis on school cultures, School Improvement literature has paid too little attention to the symbolic enactments of wealth and poverty. Many years ago in *Uses of Literacy*, Richard Hoggart (1957) articulated the cultural conflict suffered by working-class boys entering grammar schools. In many subtle ways today, vulnerable adolescents are given signals that their cultural world is alien and inferior and has no value in school. We still hear some teachers blame poor achievement on one-parent families – a category which does not seem to include their brave lone parent colleagues in the staffroom. One of my teaching students describes a teacher in his placement school, who by wearing lavish jewellery and speeding away in her shiny red car at the end of day, gives unwitting signals of her alienation from the students' lives and her impatience to get back into her own world. Fortunately, there are many excellent teachers and heads in more successful inner-city schools whose habits, relationships and conversations connect them symbolically to the lives of the community.

'Raising expectations' requires a situated understanding of the complex social dynamics of ambition and self-esteem. Teachers cannot skate over problems, but need to help youngsters to articulate their responses. Resilience is built up through a political understanding of the difficulties and opportunities. Young people growing up in poverty need to appreciate the determined hard work they will need in order to succeed. Jenny Dunn, headteacher of Seymour Park School, told me how her teachers motivated a disaffected ten-year-old to understand that his football idols required real dedication and sustained effort to succeed.

> His teacher went to watch him play on Saturdays and to talk with his coach. They worked together to motivate him. We helped him understand that you've got to have clear goals. There's a lot of glamour in football, but it's also very disciplined. They're fanatical – what you can have for your breakfast, how much sleep, lots of training. It's not like zapping a button to switch the television on. (Wrigley 2000: 40)

Cultural leadership in many schools involves a judicious balance – keeping out the worst features of antisocial or macho street behaviour while doing everything possible to make the students feel welcome, along with their neighbourhood and youth sub-cultures, complex experiences and shifting identities. Schools which force vulnerable teenagers to choose between educational success and rootedness in a community, inevitably stimulate a resistance to school which Kohl (1994) has called 'creative maladjustment'.

Understanding 'special needs'

A uniform curriculum policed by high-stakes testing inevitably constructs many individuals as inadequate. The hegemony of measurement stigmatises those who *cannot measure up*. Consequently, the school effectiveness and standards discourse undermines the struggle for greater inclusion, and, paradoxically, for higher achievement.

A complex debate is currently taking place regarding inclusion and special educational needs. We have come a long way from the days in which many children were regarded as ineducable.

The Warnock Report, using the term 'children with special educational needs' (often a temporary designation), led to the integration into mainstream schools of children who had previously been educated separately. This was a great step forward, since it helped to change the emphasis

> The Mental Deficiency Act of 1913 was the result of eugenicist agitation and it led to the incarceration of 'idiots', 'imbeciles', 'the feeble minded' and 'moral imbeciles', the last category usually referring to young people who had illegitimate children. Many were incarcerated for life in sex-segregated institutions to prevent them from reproducing. At first it was argued that units or extra classes attached to ordinary schools were best, but soon the eugenicist view prevailed and the early part of the century saw large numbers of segregated schools for 'crippled children, epileptics, educable morons and feeble minded children'. (Copeland 1997, in Rieser 2000: 132)

from defects to an identification of specific needs for support. However, even the term *needs* can send out signals of 'dependency, inadequacy and unworthiness' (Corbett 1996).

Recent theorists argue for the replacement of *medical* (or psychological) models by *social* (or environmental) ones.

> The 'medical model' sees the disabled person as the problem. We are to be adapted to fit into the world as it is . . . The emphasis is on dependence, backed up by the stereotypes of disability that call forth pity, fear and patronizing attitudes. Rather than on the needs of the person, the focus is usually on the impairment . . . 'Medical model' thinking about us pre-dominates in schools where special educational needs are thought of as emanating from the individual who is seen as different, faulty and needing to be assessed and made as normal as possible. (Rieser 2000: 119)

The social model, on the other hand:

> views the barriers that prevent disabled people from participating in any situation as being what disables them. The social model makes a funda-mental distinction between impairment and disability. *Impairment* is defined as 'the loss or limitation of physical, mental or sensory function on a long-term, or permanent basis', whereas *disability* is 'the loss or limita-tion of opportunities to take part in the normal life of the community on an equal level with others due to physical and social barriers'. (Rieser 2000: 119, citing Disabled People's International 1981)

Thus, for people with restricted mobility, a social model highlights the disabling effect of entrances without ramps and of discriminatory social attitudes. This does not mean that medical needs can be neglected: that would be like stopping a child's classmates from calling him names while failing to test his eyes or offer him glasses. The social model is becoming theoretically dominant, though there is still debate about its scope and implications. Some writers, for example, seek to make a distinction between ends and means, arguing that the provision of separate schooling is sometimes needed to prevent greater difficulties later in life.

The social model demands a reorientation of School Improvement towards the creative adaptation of schools. The *Index for Inclusion* (Booth *et al* 2000) helps set an agenda for school self-evaluation. It covers a wide range of barriers to learning, and includes material, organisational and attitudinal factors.

> **Index for Inclusion: sample questions for school review**
>
> • Are students able to participate fully in the curriculum, in clothes appropriate to their religious beliefs, for example in science and physical education?
>
> • Do staff recognise the physical effort required to complete tasks for some learners with impairments or chronic illnesses and the tiredness that can result?
>
> • Do staff recognise the mental effort expended by some students, for example using lip reading and vision aids?
>
> • Do staff recognise the additional time required by some students with impairments to use equipment in practical work?
>
> • Do staff provide alternative ways of giving experience or understanding for students who cannot engage in particular activities, for example using equipment in science, some forms of exercise in physical education, or optical science for blind students?

This requires a transformation of schools to make them more inclusive, rather than physically incorporating learners into schools which remain largely as they were. This raises the question of how much adaptation is possible within a one-size-fits-all national curriculum and given the pressures of accountability. A system which pressures teachers to ensure that the maximum number of pupils meet pre-specified objectives inevitably gives rise to a discourse of *deficit* for those who don't make it. This is not to argue for a minimalist curriculum for these pupils, but for greater flexibility.

Satirically, Crockett describes a cartoon drawing of a very small concert pianist who has to play a particular piece of music:

> As I looked at the picture, I wondered, 'what is he going to play, and how is he going to play it?' To me, the illustration epitomises the challenges of high-stakes accountability. These questions came to my mind: When can

Frederick Chopin's Opus 64, Number 1: 'The Minute Waltz', be played in 90 seconds? Who decides whether the pianist will play from an enlarged print version of the original score or from the big note 'easy piano' version? Which alterations accommodate the player and which ones modify the music? When it comes to playing this standard from the classical repertoire, just what are we asking this particular performer to do and what do we expect of him? What were the instructional goals for his performance: keyboard speed and romantic interpretation? (in O'Brien 2001: 81)

And why this piece of music at all? When the National Curriculum was introduced in England and Wales, many special needs teachers were glad that it promised a common entitlement to all learners. It has since become clear that it has many disadvantages, including denying space for a developmental curriculum in life and social skills. Inclusion and entitlement should not mean assimilation into a uniform curriculum of fixed objectives. Universal objectives invariably position many learners as defective, however careful the differentiation. The learner has little say in either the basic task or its differentiation.

> Other people's (usually non-disabled professionals') assessments of us are used to determine where we go to school; what support we get; what type of education. (Rieser 2000: 119)

A very different and more enabling approach to differentiation is to be found in education systems which are less dominated by fixed objectives. In Denmark teachers are recommended to embark upon a broad topic with a class, but with considerable choice for the students in which aspects most interest them and in how they are going to pursue them. The learner is given more control over how to learn, while developing greater self-awareness and skills of self-evaluation.

> The setting of goals and evaluation holds a work process together, both for you and for your pupils. Just as you must formulate a goal for your teaching, so must each pupil formulate a goal which will become a leading thread in the pupil's work.

> It will often happen that the learners' goals are inspired by the framework which your planning provides, and often many pupils will formulate similar objectives. However, the essential point is that each pupil or group of pupils will have ownership of the learning process and will know what they want to teach themselves, so that they can find ways of doing it more effectively. (Krogh-Jespersen et al, 1998: 17)

School exclusions

The most difficult tensions for teachers, within a generalised policy of inclusion, surround the management of disruptive behaviour. It is here that a broad definition of inclusion confronts a literal definition of *exclusion*, and in which highly charged interpersonal situations involving disorderly and even unintelligible behaviour can make even the most confident and benign teacher feel nervous, antagonistic and desperate. This is a traumatic situation: so much personal energy and professional identity is invested by teachers in maintaining the norms of schooling that it seems only natural to regard the child's behaviour as deviant and deficient rather than questioning the environment to which they fail to adapt. There is no space here to discuss specific tactics – the literature for that is extensive – but it is important to articulate the question in ways which may lead to more positive resolution. It is crucial to understand that we are dealing with structural and cultural problems rather than purely individual ones.

The introduction of market competition between schools in England led to a 450 per cent increase in the number of permanent exclusions between 1990 and 1995.

> This . . . reflects the pressures on schools to put a premium on academic success, to secure a favourable position in league tables and to ensure that the local media report on their successes and achievement. Since their funding depends on parents opting into the school, it is hard for even the most caring school to retain pupils who appear to flout its values and priorities and who may prevent other pupils from reaching targets set by the government. This is the price we are paying as a society for allowing our schools to be put into the market place and forced to tout for custom in order to survive. (Mittler 2000: 63–4)

> The dramatic rise in the number of excluded children does not reflect a sudden increase of disruptive behaviour in young people: the evidence from one major study suggests that the incidence of emotional and behavioural disorders has changed very little in 20 years (Croll and Moses 2000). What has changed is the tolerance level of the schools to pupils with disruptive behaviour. (*ibid*: 63)

It is important to counter the impression generated by the press and by one particular teacher union that exclusions are always used as a last resort, and that their main use is to protect teachers from violence. Only one per cent are for physical abuse and assaults on staff, while 30 per cent are for bullying, fighting and assaults on peers. Two thirds of permanent exclusions are for the more uncertain categories of 'disruption, misconduct and unacceptable behaviour', 'verbal abuse to staff', 'verbal abuse to peers' and 'defiance and disobedience' (National Children's Home 2000). This would suggest that we ought to be looking proactively at school ethos, not simply reacting to individual behaviour.

A quarter of schools account for two thirds of all exclusions. A pupil's chance of being excluded is not purely random and depends upon the circumstances in which he [generally a male] is growing up and being educated. It is sensible to infer that high-excluding schools may have more alternatives than they believe.

There are massive inequalities in exclusions. Despite some recent improvement, official data in Britain shows that children of African Caribbean origin are still over three times as likely to be excluded from primary school as others, and over four times as likely to be excluded from secondary schools. The pattern of stereotyping, cultural misunder-standings and blatant discrimination are clearly described by Tony Sewell (1997), Maud Blair (2001) and Chris Searle (2001). Exclusions are rising among some other ethnic groups. There is also a strong correlation between exclusion and poor reading ability and other special needs (National Children's Home 2000).

The term 'ethos' is frequently used in school improvement texts, but the impact of school ethos on behaviour needs to be better understood. Whereas a medical/psychological model looks to the individual, a social model examines the interplay between learners and environment. The case of children labelled hyperactive is telling. Researchers within a medical paradigm examine links between poor school behaviour ('atten-tion deficits' and 'hyperactivity') and chemical abnormalities, and pharmaceutical companies promote drugs such as ritalin as a direct 'cure'. The extent of prescription is not yet as high in Britain as in the USA, but there are startling differences by area. A recent Scottish survey gives a range from 1 in 300 children prescribed in some education authorities, to 1 in 30 in others, and no apparent correlation with likely contributory factors such as poverty or poor housing. In some areas, three or more children might be taking ritalin in a single class. We also need to take account of the impact of food additives on children's behaviour (see Hyperactive Children's Support Group website).

It is easy to assume that the individual child is to blame for behavioural difficulties, but if we reverse our angle of vision for a moment, we might begin to question whether schools currently provide a healthy social and educational environment for many of today's children. Perhaps we need to defer the label 'hyperactive' until we have examined whether the school is hyperpassive. Research in the United States (Flynn and Rapoport 1976) and Germany (Goetze 1992) indicates that symptoms of hyperactivity diminish with more open and active learning. More active participation helps such pupils towards more stable emotions and behaviour.

> The teachers perceive behavioural disturbances differently, and are not so negatively influenced by particular disturbances. At the same time, more open arrangements for learning offer better possibilities of direct pedagogical intervention. (Goetze 1992: 269, in Jürgens 1994)

Official responses to school exclusions have recognised their serious consequences in terms of unemployment or criminality, but have turned the pressure back onto schools. League tables for exclusions are set up to counter the impact of league tables for attainment. While trying to maintain a rigid educational environment, individuals who cannot be assimilated are inevitably at risk of exclusion, and conversely, teachers develop a negative and limited understanding of 'inclusion' as physical *containment*. A democratic orientation to school improvement must examine the impact of school climate on individual behaviour, as well as the converse.

Bilingualism – a cultural asset

Despite all the evidence across the rest of the world, monolingualism is still regarded in Britain and the USA as the norm and bilingualism as an aberration. This xenophobic perspective is profoundly damaging not only for linguistic minorities but for our whole society.

Speaking more than one language is absurdly regarded not as a bonus but as a deficit:

> Bilingualism shuts doors. It nourishes self-ghettoization, and ghettoization nourishes racial antagonism . . . Using some language other than English dooms people to second-class citizenship in American society . . . Monolingual education opens doors to the larger world . . . institutionalized bilingualism remains another source of the fragmentation of America, another threat to the dream of 'one people'. (Arthur Schlesinger Jr, 1991: 108–9, quoted by Cummins 2000)

This strange logic identifies linguistic minorities as the problem, rather than the hegemony of an anglophone power elite. Schlesinger regards the silencing of other tongues as 'nation building'; in truth, the desire to extinguish alternative cultures and world views underwrites the ignorance of the USA's political leadership whose imperial arrogance now threatens the entire world.

Here in Britain, senior government ministers talk of schools being 'swamped' by asylum seekers, so helping to stir up racial hatred against asylum seekers. Meanwhile, they are advising South Asian parents to stop using Urdu or Punjabi at home. Thus, while setting up barriers to migration – even to those fleeing from persecution – they attempt to homogenise our richly diverse population.

The use of schools to consolidate a monolingual nation at the heart of Empire has a long history. In Britain, Celtic languages were banned from schools and public life, and speakers of regional dialects were made to feel inferior.

In the early days of mass immigration from the Indian sub-continent, Asian children were isolated into special language centres, denying them immersion among first language English speakers while doing nothing to recognise the value of their mother tongue. There has been considerable progress since those days. Segregated language centres have been closed, and the terminology has changed from a discourse about 'children who can't speak English' to children who have English as an Additional Language (EAL) and 'bilingual pupils'. It is now accepted good practice to integrate newcomers as quickly as possible into mainstream classes with specialist in-class support.

A challenge to the inspection system as a result of the Stephen Lawrence enquiry has led to greater awareness. Recent inspection guidance warns against blurring EAL into SEN (special educational needs), by advising inspectors against writing such sentences as 'All pupils, including those with special educational needs and those for whom English is an additional language, achieve appropriately for their potential.' The guidelines assert that bilingualism is a valued skill (Ofsted 2002), praising lessons in which children are able to use 'short bursts of the home language'. Even this degree of recognition, however, marginalises the home language – it is implied that the major educational goal is to make it unnecessary.

Despite some recent state legislation to suppress them, the USA boasts many bilingual schools, including several hundred based on a premise of two-way immersion, i.e. where first language English speakers learn Spanish and first language Hispanics learn English. There are also many other late-exit transitional programmes. Research clearly shows the higher success of those programmes which give most support to bilingualism compared with transitional programmes which encourage the minority language only as a temporary expedient (summarised and referenced in Nieto 1998: 432; Cummins 2000). In Britain, there are still

very few multiethnic schools where the recognition of languages other
than English is other than tokenistic.

> A bridge provides access to a different shore without closing off the possi-
> bility of returning home . . .They best thing about bridges is that they do
> not need to be burned once they are used; on the contrary, they become
> more valuable with use because they help visitors from both sides become
> adjusted to different contexts.
>
> Unfortunately, however, this is a far cry from how diverse languages and
> cultures tend to be viewed in schools: the conventional wisdom is that
> if native languages and cultures are used at all, it should be only until
> one learns the important language and culture, and then they should be dis-
> carded or burned. It is definitely a one-way street with no turning back.
>
> The metaphor of the bridge suggests a different stance: You can have two
> homes, and the bridge can help you cross the difficult and conflict-laden
> spaces between them.
>
> (Nieto 1999: 115)

Jim Cummins' comprehensive survey of research demonstrates the
importance of theories of language for the School Improvement project.
He is able to refute the common sense notion that success in English
depends upon time on task, used by those who want to eliminate time
'wasted' in using the home language. He draws upon copious evidence to
back up an *interdependence* hypothesis, showing that increased fluency in
the home language correlates with the greatest gains in learning English.

> The results of virtually all evaluations of bilingual and second language
> immersion programs are consistent with predictions derived from the
> interdependence hypothesis . . . Transfer across languages of conceptual
> knowledge and academic skills (such as learning and reading strategies)
> compensates for the reduced instructional time through the majority
> language (Cummins 2000: 186).

> The study entitled School Effectiveness for Language Minority Students
> carried out by Wayne Thomas and Virginia Collier (1997) is undoubtedly
> one of the largest investigations of educational effectiveness ever con-
> ducted. It involved analysis of more than 700,000 student records com-
> piled from five large school systems during the years 1982–1996 . . . They
> report that the amount of formal schooling in L1 that students have
> received is the strongest predictor of how rapidly they will catch up aca-
> demically in L2. This factor is a stronger predictor than socioeconomic

status or the extent to which parents may or may not speak English (Cummins 2000: 223).

Cummins highlights the success of language programmes which are content-rich, i.e. where language development is integrated into academic learning of other subjects; the other major factors are students' self-esteem, a positive recognition of cultures and communities, and greater opportunities for parental involvement.

> Research results on an international scale are almost unanimous in their conclusion: children from language minority backgrounds benefit from bilingual programs when their native language plays a major role in their instruction. This is the case in countries such as Mexico, Sweden and Canada (Moorfield 1987); the Netherlands (Vallen and Stijnen 1987), the United States (Ramirez 1991; Thomas and Collier 1995) and other countries in Europe and Africa (Skutnabb-Kangas 1988).
>
> Using students' linguistic, cultural and experiential backgrounds as resources has proven to be effective in their learning . . . treating their native language ability as an advantage, encouraging them to continue their study of Spanish and staff members to learn it, and promoting in-depth approaches to affirming cultural diversity rather than superficial 'one-shot' professional development workshops or decontextualized diversity programs. (Nieto 1998: 426)

In Britain much progress has been made in supporting bilingual pupils, including multilingual displays and the employment of bilingual classroom assistants. However, we still have a long way to go in recognising and supporting languages other than English in our schools. Despite a gradual improvement, there are too few teachers from linguistic minorities even in cities such as Bradford and Birmingham. Even though Asian languages are fully recognised as foreign languages within the National Curriculum and for examinations, there is little coherent support or encouragement for children's home language development in primary schools or across the curriculum in secondary schools.

The School Improvement project needs the breadth of vision to promote linguistic diversity as a desirable national asset. It needs to incorporate into its examination of shared leadership a positive understanding of the role of bilingual assistants and teachers; they form part of the distributed intelligence of the learning organisation, with their intimate knowledge of local communities and their ability to mediate cultural differences. In a two-way relationship based on respect, they have the potential to bring the cultural riches of the community into the curriculum, as well as to help families support school learning.

'The trouble with boys'

Boys' underachievement has become the great moral panic of recent years, though the phenomenon itself is nothing new. Douglas (1964) showed that girls were outperforming boys in primary schools, but simply assumed that the boys would catch up. In most education authorities, the examinations for entry into selective secondary schools ensured that this would occur by requiring a higher pass mark for girls.

The recent data is by no means as straightforward as the headlines suggest. There is negligible difference in mathematics and science results at age 16 – two subjects which count heavily in terms of future employment prospects. The gender gap at 16 disappears by age 18, and in spite of legislation, men still tend to secure higher incomes and better promotions at work. The proportion of women pursuing IT degrees at university is small and declining (Ali 2001).

The moral panic about gender difference has served to deflect attention from social class and race. The gender gap is tiny in comparison with class differences, and between some ethnic groups (Gillborn and Mirza 2000). Girls' comparative advantage does not extend to the daughters of unskilled manual workers. In 1998, girls from social class V occupied only 1.6 per cent of university places and boys only 2 per cent (Plummer 2000: 39). While boys from professional families are surfing and their sisters swimming vigorously through the waves, the sons and daughters of unskilled manual workers still scrape along the bottom.

There is clearly an issue about raising boys' achievement, but the way in which it is framed may be counterproductive. Problems include:

* a failure to celebrate the rising achievement of both boys and girls in recent decades

* a negative stereotyping of boys in general as reluctant learners, resulting in demoralisation and defeatism rather than challenge

* the assumption that women, and particularly teachers, are to blame for boys' achievement levels

* a search for quick-fix solutions which may exacerbate the academic problem

* a refusal to address serious questions concerning norms of masculinity in our society.

By failing to question the social construction of masculinity, a deficit discourse is being created about boys which essentialises them as academic failures at the same time as accepting aggressive behaviour as 'natural' (Mahoney and Smedley 1998). As with other types of deficit discourse examined in this chapter, the underachieving male student is locked into a fixed identity of academic failure, with no attempt to challenge features of the environment which actively construct that identity – in this case, social assumptions about appropriate male behaviour. Both boys and girls suffer when macho attitudes go unchallenged within a school system which cares only about examinations.

In a period of anti-feminist backlash, women are now being blamed for the 'failure' of boys. The opposite is true, according to Victoria Foster and colleagues (Australia):

> It is not the school experience that 'feminizes' boys, but rather the ideology of traditional masculinity that keeps boys from wanting to succeed. 'The work you do here is girls' work', one school boy recently commented to a researcher. 'It's not real work.' . . . Boys eschew school work for the anti-intellectual rough and tumble; girls' achievement is inhibited by the incessant teasing and harassment of those rough and tumble boys. (Foster *et al* 2001: 14)

Whereas the women's struggle of the 1970s and 1980s contributed positively to girls' greater success, it is a residual culture of macho masculinity which is holding boys back. Boys compete on the street and in school for each other's approval, since 'manly acts of living on the edge can't just be done in isolation' (Salisbury and Jackson 1996: 219). They suffer from the stress of constantly hiding their emotions, and from the 'chronic anxiety of having to prove your manhood every second' (Foster *et al* 2001: 15).

When we theorise boys' underachievement in this way, it is easier to see the inadequacy of some of the short-term solutions proposed, including boys-only classes and a diet of war and adventure stories. We may agree that 'boys are uneasy speaking about their emotions, or reading books which express emotions', but we surely cannot concur with this state of affairs. Boys may benefit from working in pairs with girls, but we need to monitor and guide the process to ensure that they do not dominate. Attempts to raise boys' self-esteem as learners need to be modulated by an awareness of the dangers of sexist dominance.

Many recently developed ideas in response to boys' underachievement are sensible and enlightened, and will benefit girls too. For example, when teachers ask pupils to spend two minutes talking over their response with a neighbour before giving an answer to the class, this encourages many boys to think more carefully and gives less confident girls a chance to rehearse. While Bleach (1998), Frater (2000) and Hannan (1999) present some useful tactics, there are also contradictions and dangers within instrumental approaches which try to tackle lower academic achievement in isolation and do nothing to challenge the underlying ideologies of male superiority.

> It is crucial for the boys to see the folly of believing there is only one form of masculinity which is narrow, rigid and inflexible. As Lingard and Douglas (1999) claim, there is a need for the boys to be valued and affirmed as boys, but in concert with this it is also necessary to broaden the acceptable range of masculine expression available to boys. This needs to be underlined because it means teaching boys about gender in general and masculinities in particular, which requires an understanding of gender as a social construction. After Gould (1985), teaching about and to boys and young men means engaging them in the same way girls and young women have been engaged in studying women . . .

> This includes adolescent society and schoolboy customs like acting manly, conforming to a group identity, needing to belong, pressuring peers, putting down boys who are different, scapegoating, denigrating girls and anything regarded as feminine, and deriding any form of intellectualism and academic achievement. (Beckett 2001: 76)

Questions to explore in English and health education:

• What do you understand 'masculinity' to mean? What does it mean to be a man? In what ways do boys have to prove that they are men?

• How are boys expected to behave? What stereotypes are you aware of? Where do these expectations come from? Who imposes these stereotypes?

• What happens to boys if they do not behave in stereotypical ways, according to the expectations of others?

• What is homophobia and what role do you think it plays in boys' lives?

• What do you think life might be like for a member of the opposite sex?

(Wayne Martino, 2001: 92)

Virginia Foster and colleagues (2001: 17) point out that feminism has offered 'a blueprint for a new boyhood and masculinity based on a passion for justice, a love of equality, and expression of a fuller emotional palette.'

Martin Mills suggests a deconstruction or 'emasculation' of current constructions of risk taking.

> This might involve explorations of women's engagement in high-risk activities such as the suffragette movement; the anti-slave movement in the US; the women's peace movement in Australia (Pine Gap) and in the UK (Greenham Common); and also of course less sensationalized forms of risk taking such as childbirth. (Mills 2001: 62)

It is also important to be aware that homophobic taunts are part of the process by which boys police their own masculinity – a process which creates inhibitions about showing emotions, narrows the range of acceptable behaviours, and is intensely destructive of less macho boys, whether or not they identify as gay. An Ontario teachers' union reminds us of the extent of this problem, arguing that approximately one person in ten is gay or lesbian; that 30 per cent of gay youth attempt suicide at least once; and that 30 per cent of completed suicides among all youth can be attributed to issues surrounding sexual orientation (Elementary Teachers' Federation of Ontario website, which gives clear and helpful advice on helping to eliminate homophobia).

When you hear adults making ugly or malicious comments or jokes. It's important to respond. Depending on the situation, privately or publicly tell the person how such comments make you feel.

Never laugh along with people making such jokes or comments.

Don't assume everybody is heterosexual. The constant assumption of heterosexuality renders gay, lesbian, bisexual and transgender people invisible. Use examples of famous gay and lesbian people in history.

www.etfo.on.ca (links to Equity: Homophobia)

Such considerations have been sidelined into the margins of consciousness by the School Effectiveness literature. School Improvement needs to pay greater attention to the construction of gender and its intersection with social class as a crucial factor in students' self-perception as learners.

Racism and refugees

The connections between racism and educational failure are not accidental, nor are they the result of inferior intelligence or bad attitudes on the part of black children. Institutional racism, embedded structurally and culturally within our schools, actively produces the failure of Black pupils within a school system which claims to be open and inclusive. (It is salutory to recall the title of Bernard Coard's historic text *How the West Indian Child is Made Educationally Sub-normal in the British School System*, published in 1971. The processes of segregation, exclusion and failure have been described in numerous reports since.)

Patterns of unfair treatment including a disproportionate frequency of reprimands and criticisms and unwarranted reactions to cultural difference have been well documented (see, for example, Gillborn 1990, Searle 2001, Blair 2001).

> Perhaps even more significant than the frequency of criticism and controlling statements which Afro-Caribbean students received was the fact that they were often singled out for criticism even though several students of different ethnic origins were engaged in the same behaviour . . . In sum, Afro-Caribbean students were not only criticised more often than their white peers, but the same behaviour in a white pupil might not bring about criticism at all. (Gillborn 1990: 30, in Blair and Cole 2000)

Not surprisingly, this generates antagonism:

> Students were inevitably forced into highly significant face-winning, face-retaining and face-losing contests between themselves and the teachers. (Wright 1987: 111, in Blair and Cole 2000)

The situation has been exacerbated by the educational market, high-stakes assessment and accountability. The dramatic rise in school exclusions involved an extraordinary proportion of African Caribbean boys.

Some teachers construct a more positive but educationally limiting stereotype for black students as 'natural athletes but too restless to sit and learn'. Others set about celebrating Caribbean food and rhythms in a multicultural response, though this stops short of addressing the question of racism. Assumptions of parental neglect and indifference towards schooling are still widespread, as part of a deficit discourse which blames the victim.

The statistics tell a different story. Gillborn and Mirza (2000) provide evidence from one large education authority that African Caribbeans enter school more advanced but leave with the lowest levels of achievement.

Despite the alarm about failing city schools, there has been very little British research into school success for this population. Maud Blair and Jill Bourne's report (1998) has a set of key characteristics which is quite distinct from the bland and ambiguous lists to be found in most mainstream 'school effectiveness' studies. Like my own parallel study of school success for bilingual Asian students (Wrigley 2000), it has been widely read by specialists in multiethnic education but is rarely cited in the mainstream study of School Improvement in Britain, even in books which claim to illuminate the intractable problems of inner city achievement.

The education of refugees is a particularly critical issue today. Our governments mainly regard refugees as an unnecessary burden. Those who profit from arms sales, and the warmongering politicians who support them, deny responsibility for the tide of human misery they have caused. The skills and diverse experience of refugees, and their desire to contribute to the development of their country of refuge, are squandered by asylum laws which keep them marginalised and forbid them employment. The longer term benefits of immigration are overlooked in a deficit discourse reinforced by the rampant xenophobia promoted after 11 September 2001.

In the aftermath, we see leading New Labour politicians in Britain riding the bandwagon of resurgent racism. Leading government ministers incite racial hatred by feeding the media soundbites that refugees are swamping our schools, then pass new laws to incarcerate the children in detention centres. Courageous teachers in schools which have positively welcomed refugees know the problem lies elsewhere: the market system of accountability positions the victims of poverty and discrimination as an obstacle to its ruthless drive to raise standards. The pursuit of higher and higher targets clearly has no place for human suffering, and no time for children whose needs weigh upon the cost side of the balance sheet of efficiency. Children have become units of value addedness for the statisticians, rather than schools adapting to meet their needs.

Asylum seekers are a major stumbling block for a narrow-minded accountability discourse. The sophisticated statistics of School Effectiveness cannot begin to calculate their complex needs or measure their schools' efficiency in 'adding value'; the process theories of mainstream School Improvement are far too general to deal with the creation of welcoming educational environments for the traumatised children of war.

There has been rapid development of theory and practical understanding by writers such as Jill Rutter (2000), adding a valuable new dimension to the literatures of equality, race and bilingualism. School Improvement is failing in its moral responsibility, as well as in its narrower aims of raising achievement, if it pretends that this is none of its business. We need to ask, insistently: Is there a connection between school improvement and social justice? Where is the vision we have heard so much about?

CHAPTER ELEVEN

Schools for a future

The moment I understand history as possibility, I must also understand education in a different way.

(Antonia Darder, 2002: x)

A story is told that the band continued to play in the ballroom of the Titanic while the ship was starting to sink. The mighty ocean liner was well ahead of schedule, and its officers racing to beat a performance target, so perhaps we should regard colliding with an iceberg as a minor blemish on otherwise excellent leadership.

When I emerge from the latest book on school improvement to switch on the news, I cannot help feeling that something doesn't quite measure up. Famine hits East Africa, schoolchildren in Iraq wonder if bombs will drop tonight, a Palestinian child is shot dead for throwing stones at the tanks which occupy his town . . . nearer home, young beggars sleep rough in sub-zero temperatures, another factory closes, and a third of our children grow up below the poverty line . . . I can't help wondering how School Improvement relates to all this.

Schools of hope? Hope isn't easy these days – an inane smile would pass for madness. It takes real courage to believe that our words and actions can make a difference – whether we are trying to improve a school, relieve poverty or stop a war. We need to defy the pessimists, to challenge the indifferent and to gather allies though their morale is low. We need to think critically and creatively, and discuss our strategy in a joined-up way.

Vision and values? We need them now more than ever. The situation we face, so early in the new millennium, requires fresh thinking about educational change. School development needs creativity, integrity and hope – a rethinking of the whole project. Leadership is, above all else, a question of deciding which direction to take.

*   *   *

175

School Improvement is at a crossroads. It has developed new metaphors for change management, abandoned linear models to embrace complexity, debated whether vision comes first or later; it has transacted and transformed, restructured and recultured, distributed leadership and internalised school review. There is an unspoken rule, however – not to think too hard about educational aims.

A strange feeling of disorientation comes over me when I spend too many hours reading some Improvement literature. Even when the title promises a more historical approach, the attempt to locate school change in time and place is rarely sustained beyond the opening chapter. The political pressures of target setting and accountability is mentioned, perhaps, as an unfortunate obstacle in the way of authentic change, but there is no sustained attempt to analyse which way our educational ship is being driven.

Behind a surface tone of exhortation, the texts are often shadowy. Words such as vision and values are never all they seem. Like ghosts, they disintegrate when we try to take hold of them. *Vision* so often comes to mean organisational adjustment. Talk about *values* soon collapses into 'valuing higher attainment' or 'valuing good behaviour', referring back into the schooling process rather than connecting outwards and forwards into the futures we would like to inhabit. Ideas and ideals collapse so easily into the performance outcomes of test scores.

It is important to reflect on how key words are used. *Change* is almost an end in itself, a way of coping with the random shifts of the school environment. *Capacity* is a troubled term: while academics relate it to complex models of culture and co-operation within a dynamic learning organisation, to many teachers it sounds like a demand to accommodate more and more top-down initiatives or the escalating targets of the accountability machine.

What if our schools need a change of *direction* as much as a boost in *capacity*?

Schools of hope in the inner city

The unrelenting pressure to 'improve' schools – along with the denial that we should begin to *rethink* them – has been particularly damaging for schools in high-poverty areas, whether in the inner city or on the public housing estates of the city's edge. Higher achievement is needed in these schools more than anywhere, but they are precisely the schools which have gained least from the improvement drive of recent years.

It is necessary also to consider more sophisticated strategies for students in disadvantaged situations, in particular applying what we know about student motivation and resilience. With all the interest in accountability and academic achievement, good intentions can easily backfire.

I would hypothesize that the greater the emphasis on academic achievement through high stakes accountability, the greater the gap becomes between advantaged and disadvantaged students. The main reason for this is that poor performing students do not need more pressure, they need greater *attachment to the school* and *motivation to want to learn*. Pressure by itself in this situation actually demotivates poor performing students.

(Fullan 1999: 19, my emphasis)

Improvement as intensification merely exaggerates the traditional barriers to learning. Fullan's focus on *attachment to the school* and *motivation to learn* finds echoes in some of the more heretical writers: Sergiovanni's emphasis on community; MacBeath, Rudduck and Fielding on student voice; the insistence on authentic learning which runs through the great coalitions of Essential and Accelerated Schools in North America. It connects too with Maud Blair's analysis of leadership and ethos in multiethnic schools, and my earlier use of the word *empowerment* – a much abused term – to characterise an orientation to learning, community and school development which is based on inclusion and equality.

The complexity of inner city schools cannot be understood from a narrow research platform; we need a better sense of context, a wider conceptual base, and a serious commitment to social justice. David Hopkins and David Jackson correctly state that research into the development paths of schools in different socio-economic contexts is 'not well trodden territory' (2003: 93). A major error is to pursue capacity as a substitute for getting to grips with context (as, for example, in Hopkins' otherwise outstanding book *School Improvement for Real*, 2001).

The issue of *attachment* to school needs to be thought through in terms of the school as community and its relationship with wider communities. The more troubled a student's social life may be outside of school – and let us not make any simplistic generalisations about 'dysfunctional working-class neighbourhoods' – the more important it becomes to develop a school environment which is comfortable, inviting and stimulating, a *house for learning*. It is futile to bemoan a lack of social capital while failing to create schools which promote it. The recent emphasis on reculturing within the Improvement literature needs to be contextualised so as to take account of parental and community perceptions, as well as students' involvement in school evaluation and transformation.

Social justice has to be integral to the project of improving schools. This is true even when we are looking, in a narrow sense, at attainment: the PISA 2000 study shows almost all countries scoring equally in terms of their higher attainers, but differing in their average attainment levels because of wide differences at the lower end of the scale (see Deutsches PISA-Konsortium 2001: 388). The general exhortation to raise expectations needs to be reframed in terms of a cultural struggle for the meaning of school learning and for personal and collective futures. Student identities and achievements, and the processes by which personal and social development is evaluated, should be re-examined and re-articulated in a spirit of hope, not measured against pre-defined 'standards'. This requires a serious challenge to discourses of deficit, and an insistence on seeing disadvantaged children as *at promise* rather than *at risk*.

Confusion has been sown by overreliance on the handful of research studies selectively highlighted within the School Effectiveness tradition. Such research emphasises a narrow 'back to basics' curriculum combined with tightly scripted instruction and a strict disciplinary regime. A more substantial research base points in other directions, for example:

- an emphasis on authentic curriculum and pedagogy, and cognitive challenge, in extensive networks of schools in the USA (see the summaries of research on the Coalition of Essential Schools and Accelerated Schools Project websites)

- well established patterns of constructivist learning in successful multi-ethnic schools in Britain (Wrigley 2000, also 2000a)

- the cooperative and community-supported learning in the small rural schools of the Escuela Nueva movement in Columbia and elsewhere (Dalin 1994).

Rather than a singular emphasis on literacy as technical competence, a better way forward would be to combine intensive periods of practice and explicit instruction with a curriculum of meaningful cooperative activities.

Even if it could be proved that rigorous instruction were more 'effective', according to whatever narrow performance measures, this would still represent a highly problematic strategy for school improvement. Andy Hargreaves points to the danger of an apartheid model of school development in countries like England. While schools in more advantaged areas are being granted greater flexibility to develop as learning communities which prepare their students for the 'knowledge society', others will instruct their students for limited short-term gains in preparation for a low-level service role.

> Schools and teachers in poor communities in the desolate sprawl of housing estates ... struggle in the shadow of impending failure – watchful of test scores, fearful of intervention and with a bellyful of imposed restrictions and requirements ... They teach the basic skills of maths and literacy that get their students to improve up to a point in primary school only to see their achievements plateau in the high-school years ... Students learn not to create knowledge, develop ingenuity or solve unfamiliar problems in flexible formats; their destiny is to be literate and numerate enough to serve and support the 'weightless work' of their affluent superiors in restaurants, tourist hotels, health spas, and other service work where understanding instructions, communicating obsequiously and urging others to have a nice day, have far greater importance than inventiveness or ingenuity. (Hargreaves 2003: 191)

Schools of hope in a troubled world

The complex set of processes known as *globalisation* creates unprecedented challenges for education. Confusion arises because the term conflates conflicting emphases. While a depoliticised interpretation stresses the revolution in ICT, faster knowledge transfer and a greater cultural mix, more critical writers point to the consequences of a dramatic concentration of economic and political power. Globalisation is better understood not as something qualitatively different but as the culmination of a long historical development – 'capitalism reaching maturity' (Wood 1998: 47).

> [Globalization is] the process whereby capitalism is increasingly constituted on a transnational basis, not only in the trade of goods and services but, even more important, in the flow of capital and the trade in currencies and financial instruments. The dominant players in the globalization are the world's few hundred largest private corporations, which have increasingly integrated production and marketing across national borders over the past decade. (McChesney 1998: 1)

The consequences are felt on a planetary scale. 'Development' means the transformation of peasants into wage labourers, a switch in land use away from basic food production and towards export crops, and an insupportable debt for misdirected development aid received earlier. A world economy geared towards fulfilling capitalism's drive to maximise production and consumption leads to ecological crisis and global warming. The concentration of economic power in a few multinational corporations and states, particularly the USA, leads directly to imperialist domination and wars for oil.

In this context, Marx's prognosis of a division of society into the two powerful classes of capital and wage workers is reaching fruition on a global scale. The confusing category 'middle class' covers many white-collar and professional workers whose lives are increasingly insecure, and who are, in reality, simply a different kind of wage labourer. While manual workers' children are the worst victims of the current intensification drive in schools, the children of other types of workers are also damaged. As learning is reduced to an accumulation of examinable knowledge, critical understanding becomes increasingly difficult for all young people.

All children are affected by the commodification of pleasure:

> Capitalism requires that free-of-charge happiness be [replaced with] what can be bought and sold. (Dowbor 1997: 26)

and by the destruction of freely available resources

> clean rivers, air, drinking water, chemical-free food, free time, and the space for adults and children to socialize freely (Darder 2002: 40).

This has the effect that 'the notion of society as a collection of possessive individuals is reinforced and any serious sense of the common good is marginalized' (*ibid*: 11).

At the same time, the mass media saturate our consciousness with authorised interpretations of events. For months on end (February 2003) the news media have distributed daily soundbites about suspected 'weapons of mass destruction' in Iraq, as if America and Britain were armed with waterpistols. Every night on television, the iconic face of Saddam Hussein substitutes for the men, women and children of Iraq, as if he alone will die when hell rains down on Baghdad. These interpretations of history are being challenged at street stalls, on demonstrations and some newspapers while our schools are too busy covering the exam syllabus. Through this vast educational process, an assertion of hope and common humanity, globalization may have reached a turning point in the participation of 10,000,000 people across the world in demonstrations against war on February 15 – an event unprecedented in the whole of human history.

All this requires from us a more daring sense of moral purpose, vision and values than hitherto. Vision has to go to the roots of educational provision and processes. This chapter can do no more than give some pointers.

- Hargreaves and Fullan (1998: 42) suggest that 'schools are one of our last hopes for rebuilding a sense of community'. Since structure constrains culture, we need to take seriously the restructuring as well as the reculturing of schools. The models developed by the Coalition of Essential Schools, experimental schools in Germany such as Bielefeld's Laborschule (Laboratory School), and schools in Denmark and Norway merit our serious attention.

- Critical thinking, critical literacy and media education need to be centrally located in any 21st century curriculum. This is very different from the pre-packaged Thinking Skills programmes currently being promoted in the name of the knowledge society.

- New forms of situated and concerned learning need to be developed, including community-based projects. For most young people, the postmodern skimming of consciousness by the rapid flashing of media images is paralleled, not challenged, by a drizzle of inert information bytes in school. We have to create new kinds of learning community in which students are

  > not to be seen merely as an audience but as part of a community of common concern in which one hopes to participate constructively. (Chomsky 2000: 21)

- To support the necessary change, new forms of professional development need to be established which combine the generation of critical understanding with the sharing of practical support. The role of loose but creative networks and coalitions built around a few common principles provides one model (see, for example, Coalition of Essential Schools). The pioneering role of the teachers' cooperative Rethinking Schools, with its newspaper, books, on-line resources and conferencing, provides another. Similar networks could be built in other countries through alliances of subject associations, teacher unions and other campaigning groups, and would help to generate a counterweight to government pressures.

- Finally, we need to overcome the traditionally apolitical stance of school improvement theory. There are signs that this is beginning to happen. Ideas such as school self-evaluation and student voice in Britain (MacBeath, Ruddock, Fielding) connect to Scandinavian developments in democratic schooling. The recent emphasis on distributed leadership' (Harris and others) also has democratic potential, though it easily collapses into a simple delegation of management tasks. The concern of Grace, Duignan, Day and others for schooling as moral development and to understand the dilemmas in headship will bear fruit provided that morality isn't restricted to immediate face-to-face relationships. Fullan's concern for moral purpose now shows a greater understanding of the struggle for equity. We need to give direction by focusing on democracy, values, social justice and inclusion, and active and concerned citizenship.

Schools of hope

So much of our thinking about school improvement has been within the bounds of the politically acceptable. It is remarkable how closely its dominant tropes map onto those of capitalist society in general:

- the myth that all schools are individually capable of high levels of success, regardless of systemic inequality, if only they were properly led, echoes the Victorian 'self-made man' – that rare specimen of the entrepreneur who makes his way from rags to riches.

- learning as the 'banking' of knowledge (Freire) to be quantified and accounted for, and where the producers of knowledge are constantly monitored against how much they have 'added value'

- the concept of curriculum as externally imposed and fixed, just as the industrial worker receives instructions to produce goods to a set design for distant customers

- the pupils' sense of reward as extrinsic to the task, and of learning seen as exchange value divorced from use value and which is separate from the emotions, creativity and personal meaning-making of the worker

- the leader as site manager, an accountable agent within a project which is determined by powerful forces higher up the chain of command.

We need to think outside this frame, and reconnect school improvement to a wider set of social values which might transcend the present captive state of our world. We need a sense of leadership as *direction finding*, not just capacity building. We need a fuller sense of transformative leadership which connects up with dynamic *social transformation*. We need to *turn around* our schools until they engage with the contradictions, the hopes and fears of local communities. We need a sense of *achievement* which looks beyond the accumulation of factual knowledge, which links hand, heart and mind and involves a moral engagement with the whole of humanity. We need new concepts of intelligence – distributed, emotional, cultural, political – which involve our engagement in shaping the future of our planet. We need the courage to challenge political decisions which place a ceiling on achievement, whether these are new forms of school selection or student debt or punitive accountability regimes which drive good teachers out of needy schools.

We need commitment to a better future.

We have to be visionary.

We must dare to dream.

We will have to *rethink education*, and not simply 'improve' schools.

References

Accelerated Schools Project. www.acceleratedschools.net

Adey P. and Shayer M. (1994) *Really raising standards*. London: Routledge

Alderson P. (2000) Practising democracy in two inner city schools. In Osler A. (ed) *Citizenship and democracy in schools: diversity, identity, equality*. Stoke on Trent: Trentham

Ali L. (2001) Women in information technology. *Improving Schools* 4(2)

Altrichter H., Schley W. and Schratz M. (1998) *Handbuch zur Schulentwicklung*. Innsbruck: StudienVerlag

Angus L. (1993) The sociology of school effectiveness. *British Journal of Sociology of Education* 14(3)

Apple M. (1993) *Official knowledge: democratic education in a conservative age*. London: Routledge

Apple M. (1996) *Cultural politics and education*. Buckingham: Open University Press

August S. and Hakuta K. (eds) (1997) *Improving schooling for language-minority children: a research agenda*. National Research Council, Institute of Medicine (US) National Academy Press

Ball S. (1990). *Politics and policy making in education – explorations in policy sociology*. London: Routledge

Ball S. (1998) Educational studies, policy entrepreneurship and social theory. In Slee R and Weiner G. (eds) *School effectiveness for whom?* London: Falmer

Barker Lunn L. C. (1970) *Streaming in the primary school*. Slough: NFER

Barnes D. (1969) Language in the secondary classroom. In Barnes D. *et al*: *Language, the learner and the school*. Harmondsworth: Penguin

BASRC (Bay City School Reform Collaborative) (1999) Equity Brief. www.basrc.org/Pubs&Docs/EquityBriefOct99.pdf

Baumert J. and Schümer G. (2002) Family background, selection and achievement: the German experience. *Improving Schools* 5(3)

Beckett L. (2001) Challenging boys: addressing issues of masculinity within a gender equity framework. In Martino W. and Meyenn B. (eds) *What about the boys?* Buckingham: Open University Press

Bennett N. (2001) Power, structure and culture: an organizational view of school effectiveness and school improvement. In Harris A. and Bennett N. (eds) *School effectiveness and school improvement: alternative perspectives*. London: Continuum

186   SCHOOLS OF HOPE

Bentley T. (2001) The creative society: reuniting schools and lifelong learning. In Fielding M. (ed) *Taking education really seriously: four years' hard Labour*. London: RoutledgeFalmer

BERA (2001) Report on methodological seminar on Hay/McBer enquiry into teacher effectiveness: 9 May 2001. *Research Intelligence* 76

Berliner D. (1993) *Educational reform in an era of disinformation*. Education Policy Analysis Archives 1(2) //epaa.asu.edu/epaa/v1n2.html

Biddle B. (1997) Foolishness, dangerous nonsense, and real correlates of state differences in achievement. www.pdkintl.org/kappan/kbid9709.htm

Bildungskommission NRW (1995) *Zukunft der Bildung – Schule der Zukunft*. Denkschrift der Kommission 'Zukunft der Bildung – Schule der Zukunft' beim Ministerpräsidenten des Landes Nordrhein-Westfalen. Neuwied

Black P. *et al* (2002) *Working inside the black box: assessment for learning in the classroom*. London: King's College

Blair M. (2001) *Why pick on me? School exclusion and black youth*. Stoke on Trent: Trentham

Blair M. and Bourne J. (1998) *Making the difference: teaching and learning strategies in successful multi-ethnic schools*. Sudbury: DfEE/Open University

Blair M. and Cole M. (2000) Racism and education: the imperial legacy. In Cole M. (ed) *Education, equality and human rights*. London: RoutledgeFalmer

Blase J. *et al* (1995) *Democratic principals in action: eight pioneers*. London: Sage

Bleach K. (ed) (1998) *Raising boys' achievement in schools*. Stoke on Trent: Trentham

Booth T. (2000) *Index for inclusion: developing learning and participation in schools*. Bristol: CSIE

Boring E. G. (1923) Intelligence as the tests test it. *New Republic* 34

Bourdieu P. (1990) *The logic of practice*. Cambridge: Polity Press

Bourdieu P. (1999) *The weight of the world*. (Postscript) Cambridge: Polity Press

Bourdieu P. and Passeron J-C. (1977) *Reproduction in education, society and culture*. London: SAGE [original French edition 1970]

Brighouse T. (2002) – see Tumber A. and Foley J. Birmingham – the Brighouse years. *Improving Schools* 5(2)

Brown D. (2000) Implementing citizenship education in a primary school. In Osler A. (ed) *Citizenship and democracy in schools: diversity, identity, equality*. Stoke on Trent: Trentham

Büeler X. (1998) Schulqualität und Schulwirksamkeit. In Altrichter H. *et al* (eds) *Handbuch zur Schulentwicklung*. Innsbruck: StudienVerlag

Burbules N. and Torres C. (eds) (2000) *Globalization and education: critical perspectives*. London: Routledge

Burgess T. (1980) What makes an effective schcool? In Tizard B. *et al* (1980) *Fifteen thousand hours – a discussion*. London: Institute of Education

Burt C. (1937) *The backward child*. London: University of London Press

Burtonwood N. (1986) *The culture concept in educational studies*. Windsor: NFER-Nelson

Busher H. (2001) The micro-politics of change, improvement and effectiveness in schools. In Harris A. and Bennett N. (eds) *School effectiveness and school improvement: alternative perspectives*. London: Continuum

Carey J. (1992) *The intellectuals and the masses: pride and prejudice among the literary intelligentsia 1880–1939*. London: Faber & Faber

Carter C. (2000) Meeting the challenge of inclusion; human rights eduction to improve reltionships in a boys' secondary school. In Osler A. (ed) (2000) *Citizenship and democracy in schools: diversity, identity, equality*. Stoke on Trent: Trentham

Chitty C. (2001) IQ, racism and the eugenics movement. *Forum* 43(3)

Chomsky N. (2000) *Chomsky on miseducation*. Lanham Maryland: Rowman and Littlefield

Claire H. (2001) *Not aliens: primary school children and the Citizenship/PSHE curriculum*. Stoke on Trent: Trentham

Clarke P. (2001) Feeling compromised – the impact on teachers of the performance culture. *Improving Schools* 4(3)

Coalition of Essential Schools. www.essentialschools.org

Coard B. (1971) *How the West Indian child is made educationally subnormal in the British school system*. London: New Beacon Books

Cole M. and Engeström Y. (1993) A cultural-historical approach to distributed cognition. In Salomon G. (ed) *Distributed cognitions: psychological and educational considerations*. Cambridge: Cambridge University Press

Coleman J. S. *et al* (1966) *Equality of educational opportunity*. Washington DC: Government Printing Office

Cooper B. (1976) *Bernstein's codes: a classroom study*. Brighton: University of Sussex

Copeland I. (1997) Pseudo-science and dividing practices: a genealogy of the first educational provision for pupils with learning difficulties. *Disability and Society* 12 (5)

Corbett J. (1996) *Bad-mouthing: the language of special needs*. London: Falmer

Cowburn W. (1986) *Class, ideology and community education*. London: Croom Helm

Croll P. (1983) Transfer and pupil performance. In Galton M. and Willcocks J. (eds) *Moving from the primary classroom*. London: RKP

Cullingford C. (ed) (1999) *An inspector calls: Ofsted and its effects on school standards*. London: Kogan Page

Cummins J. (2000) *Language, power and pedagogy: bilingual children in the crossfire*. Clevedon: Multilingual Matters

188   SCHOOLS OF HOPE

Dalin P. (1998) Developing the Twenty-First Century School. In Hargreaves A. *et al* (eds) *International handbook of educational change*. Dordrecht: Kluwer

Dalin P. *et al* (1994) *How schools improve – an international report*. London: Cassell

Darder A. (2002) *Reinventing Paulo Freire – a pedagogy of love*. Boulder, Colo: Westview Press

Darling-Hammond L. (1991) *The implications of tesing policy for quality and equality*. Phi Delta Kappan 73(3)

Davies M. and Edwards G. (2001) Will the curriculum caterpillar ever learn to fly? In Fielding M. (ed) *Taking education really seriously: four years hard Labour*. London: RoutledgeFalmer

Day C. (1995) Leadership and professional development: developing reflective practice. In Busher H. and Saran R. (eds) *Managing Teachers as Professionals in Schools*. London: Kogan Page

Day C. *et al* (2000) *Leading schools in times of change*. Buckingham: Open University Press

Delamont S. (1983) Teachers and their specialist subjects. In Galton M. and Willcocks J. (eds) *Moving from the primary classroom*. London: RKP

Deutsches PISA-Konsortium (ed) (2001) *PISA 2000: Basiskompetenzen von Schülerinnen und Schülern im internationalen Vergleich*. Opladen: Leske u. Budrich

DfEE (1997) *The implementation of the National Literacy Strategy*. London: HMSO

DfES (compiled annually) 'Autumn Package'
www.standards.dfes.gov.uk/performance/ap/index.html

Dickens C. (1854) *Hard Times*

Douglas J.W.B.(1964) *The home and the school*. London: MacGibbon and Kee

Dowbor L. (1997) *Preface: Pedagogy of the heart, by Paulo Freire*. New York: Continuum

Dreiger D. (1989) *The last Civil Rights Movement*. London: Hurst

Dweck C. (2002) Beliefs that make smart people dumb. In Sternberg R. (ed) *Why smart people can be so stupid*. New Haven: Yale University Press

Eagleton T. (1983) *Literary theory: an introduction*. Oxford: Blackwell

Education Queensland (2000) New Basics curriculum. www.education.qld.gov.au

Elementary Teachers' Federation of Ontario, see www.etfo.on.ca

Engeström Y. and Middleton D. (eds) (1996) *Cognition and communication at work*. Cambridge: Cambridge University Press

European Round Table of Industrialists (1994) *Education for Europeans: towards a learning society*. Brussels: ERT Education Policy Group

Fielding M. (1999) Target setting, policy pathology and student perspectives: learning to labour in new times. *Cambridge Journal of Education* 29(2)

Fielding M. (ed) (2001a) *Taking Education Really Seriously: Four Years Hard Labour*. London: RoutledgeFalmer

Fielding M. (ed) (2001b) Special edition: Student Voice. *Forum* 43(2)

Fielding M. (2001c) Ofsted, inspection and the betrayal of democracy. *Journal of Philosophy of Education* 35(4)

Fink D. (2001) The two solitudes: policy makers and policy implementers. In Fielding M. (ed) (2001) *Taking Education Really Seriously: Four Years Hard Labour.* London: RoutledgeFalmer

Flynn J. R. (1999) Searching for justice: the discovery of IQ gains over time. *American Psychologist* 54, pp. 5–20

Flynn W. M. and Rapoport J. L. (1976) Hyperactivity in open and traditional classroom environments. *Journal of Special Education* 10

Foster V., Kimmel M. and Skelton C. (2001) 'What about the boys?' an overview of the debates. In Martino W. and Meyenn B. (eds) *What about the boys? Issues of masculinity in schools.* Buckingham: Open University Press

Francis H. (1980) A question of method. In Tizard B. *et al* (1980) *Fifteen thousand hours – a discussion.* London: Institute of Education

Frater G. (2000) *Securing boys' literacy: a survey of effective practice in primary schools.* London: Basic Skills Agency

Freire P. (1974) *Education: the practice of freedom.* London: Writers and Readers' Publishing Cooperative

Freire P. (1994) *Pedagogy of the oppressed.* New York: Continuum

Freire P. (1998) *Teachers as cultural workers: letters to those who dare to teach.* Boulder, Colo: Westview

Fullan M. (1993) *Change forces.* London: Falmer

Fullan M. (1999) *Change forces – the sequel.* London: Falmer

Gardner H. (1993) *Frames of mind: the theory of multiple intelligences.* London: Fontana

Gardner H., Kornhaber M. and Wake W. (1996) *Intelligence: multiple perspectives.* Fort Worth: Harcourt Brace

Gatto J. T. (1992) *Dumbing us down: the hidden curriculum of compulsory schooling.* Gabriola Island BC: New Society Publishers

Gillborn D. (1990) *'Race', ethnicity and education.* London: Unwin Hyman

Gillborn D. and Mirza H. (2000) Educational inequality: mapping race, class and gender. www.ofsted.gov.uk

Goetze H. (1992) 'Wenn Freie Arbeit schwierig wird . . .' – Stolperstein auf dem Weg zum Offenen Unterricht. In Reiss G. and Eberle G. (eds) *Offener Unterricht – Freie Arbeit mit lernschwachen Schülerinnen und Schülern.* Weinheim

Gould M. (1985) Teaching about men and masculinity. Method and meaning. *Teaching sociology* 12(4)

Grace G. (1995) *School leadership: beyond educational management.* London: Falmer

Grace G. (1998) Realizing the mission: Catholic approaches to school effectiveness. In Slee R. and Weiner G. (eds) *School effectiveness for whom?* London: Falmer

Gunter H. (2001) *Leaders and leadership in education.* London: Chapman

Hallinger P. and Murphy J. (1986) The social context of effective schools. *American Journal of Education* 94

Hannan G. (1999) *Improving boys' performance.* London: Folens

Hargreaves A. (1994) *Changing teachers, changing times.* London: Cassell

Hargreaves A. (2003) Professional learning communities and performance training cults: the emerging apartheid of school improvement. In Harris A. *et al. Effective leadership for school improvement.* London: RoutledgeFalmer

Hargreaves A. and Fullan M. (1998) *What's worth fighting for in education?* Buckingham: Open University Press

Hargreaves A., Lieberman A., Fullan M. and Hopkins D. (eds) (1998) *International handbook of educational change.* Dordrecht: Kluwer

Harris A. (2002) Distributed leadership in schools: leading or misleading? BELMAS Conference (Birmingham), keynote paper

Harris A. and Bennett N. (eds) (2001) *School effectiveness and school improvement – alternative perspectives.* London: Continuum

Hatcher R. (1998) Social justice and the politics of school effectiveness and school improvement. *Race, ethnicity and education* 1

Hatcher R. (2001) Privatisation and schooling. In Clyde C. and Simon B. (eds) *Promoting comprehensive education in the 21st Century.* Stoke on Trent: Trentham

Herdegen P. (2001) *Demokratische Bildung.* Donauwörth: Auer

Hill C. (1965) *Intellectual origins of the English Revolution.* Oxford: Oxford University Press

HMI (2001) National Literacy Strategy: the third year. (www.ofsted.gov.uk)

HMI (2001b) Providing for gifted and talented children: an evaluation of Excellence in Cities and other grant-funded programmes

Hoggart R. (1957) *The uses of literacy.* London: Chatto & Windus

Hopkins D. (1998) Introduction: Tensions in and prospects for school improvement. In Hargreaves A. *et al* (eds) *International handbook of educational change.* Dordrecht: Kluwer

Hopkins D. (2001) *School improvement for real.* London: RoutledgeFalmer

Hopkins D. and Jackson D. (2003) Building the capacity for leading and learning. In Harris A. *et al*: Effective leadership for school improvement. London: RoutledgeFalmer

Humphreys L. (1989) Intelligence: three kinds of instability and their consequences for policy. In Linn R. L. (ed) *Intelligence: measurement, theory and public policy.* Chicago: University of Illinois

Hunt G. (2001) Democracy or a command curriculum: teaching literacy in England. *Improving Schools* 4(3)

Improving Schools, vols 1–5 (1998–2002) Stoke on Trent: Trentham

Inglis F. (1989) Managerialism and morality. In Carr W. (ed) *Quality in teaching: arguments for a reflective professional*. London: Falmer

Inglis F. (2000) A malediction upon management. *Journal of Education Policy* 15(4)

Ireson J. and Hallam S. (2001) *Ability grouping in education*. London: Chapman

Jamieson I. and Wikeley F. (2001) A contextual perspective: fitting round the school needs of students. In Harris A. and Bennett N. (eds) *School effectiveness and school improvement – alternative perspectives*. London: Continuum

Johnson R. (1979) 'Really useful knowledge'. In Clarke J. *et al* (eds) *Working-class culture – studies in history and theory*. London: Hutchinson

Jowett S. and Baginsky M. (1991) *Building bridges: parental involvement in schools*. Slough: NFER-Nelson

Joyce B., Calhoun E. and Hopkins D. (1997) *Models of learning – tools for teaching*. Buckingham: Open University Press

Joyce B., Calhoun E. and Hopkins D. (1999) *The new structure of school improvement*. Buckingham: Open University Press

Jürgens E. (1994) *Die 'neue' Reformpädagogik und die Bewegung Offener Unterricht*. Sankt Augustin: Akademia

Keddie N. (1971) Classroom knowledge. In Young M. F. D. (ed) *Knowledge and control*. London: Collier-Macmillan

Kemmis S., Cole P. and Suggett D. (1983) *Orientations to curriculum and transition: towards the socially-critical school*. Melbourne: Victorian Institute of Secondary Education

Kenway J. (2001) Keynote speech, ICSEI (Toronto), summarised in *Improving Schools* 4(1)

Kenway J. and Bullen E. (2001) *Consuming children: education-entertainment-advertising*. Buckingham: Open University Press

Klein N. (2000) *No logo*. London: Flamingo

Klein R. (2001) An editor visits – Millfields Community School, Hackney. *Improving Schools* 4(3)

Knapp M. S., Shields P. M. and Turnbull B. J. (1995) *Academic challenge in high-poverty classrooms*. Phi Delta Kappan 76(10)

Kohl H. (1994) *'I won't learn from you' and other thoughts on creative maladjustment*. New York: New Press

Krogh-Jespersen K., Methling A. B. and Striib A. (1998) *Inspiration til undervisnings-differentiering*. Copenhagen: Undervisningsministeriet (Folkeskoleafdelingen)

Kutnick P., Blatchford P. and Baines E. (2002) Pupil groupings in primary school classrooms: sites for learning and social pedagogy? *British Educational Research Journal* 28(2)

Labov W. (1969) *The logic of nonstandard English*. Georgetown Monographs on Language and Linguistics, vol 22

Lauder H., Jamieson I. and Wikeley F. (1998) Models of effective schools: limits and capabilities. In Slee R. and Weiner G. (eds) *School effectiveness for whom?* London: Falmer

Lave J. and Wenger E. (1991) *Situated learning: legitimate peripheral participation*. Cambridge: Cambridge University Press

Lawton D. *et al* (1978) *Theory and practice of curriculum studies*. London: Routledge

League of Professional Schools. www.coe.uga.edu/lps

Leat D. (1998) *Thinking through geography*. Cambridge: Chris Kington

Levacic R. and Woods P. (2002) Raisiing school performance in the league tables. *British Educational Research Journal* 28(2)

Levin H. (1998) Accelerated schools: a decade of evolution. In Hargreaves A. *et al* (eds) *International Handbook of Educational Change*. Dordrecht: Kluwer

Lingard B. and Douglas P. (1999) *Men engaging feminisms*. Buckingham: Open University Press

Lingard B., Ladwig J. and Luke A. (1998) School effects in postmodern conditions. In Slee R. and Weiner G. (eds) *School effectiveness for whom? Challenges to the school effectiveness and school improvement movements*. London: Falmer

Lodge C. (2002) 'Learning is something you do to children': discourses of learning and student empowerment. *Improving Schools* 5(1)

Luke A. (1999) Education 2010 and New Times: why equity and social justice still matter, but differently. //education.qld.gov.au/corporate/newbasics/docs/onlineal.doc

Luke A. (2001) Keynote speech at New Curriculum for the Knowledge Age conference. Summary at www.curriculum.edu.au/conference/2001/2001conf/summary4.htm

MacBeath J. (1999) *Schools must speak for themselves; the case for school self-evaluation*. London: Routledge

MacBeath J. with Schratz M., Meuret D. and Jakobsen L. (2000) *Self-evaluation in European schools*. London: RoutledgeFalmer

MacBeath J. and McGlynn A. (2002) *Self-evaluation: what's in it for schools?* London: RoutledgeFalmer

MacBeath J. and Sugimine H. (2003) *Self-evaluation in the global classroom*. London: RoutledgeFalmer

McChesney R. (1998) The political economy of global communication. In McChesney R. *et al* (eds) *Capitalism and the information age*. New York: Monthly Review Press

MacGilchrist B. *et al* (1997) *The intelligent school*. London: Chapman

Mahony P. and Smedley S. (1998) New times, old panics: the underachievement of boys. *Change: transformations in education*. University of Sydney 1(2)

Mahony P. and Hextall I. (2000) *Reconstructing teaching: standards, performance and accountability*. London: RoutledgeFalmer

Maitles H. (2001) What type of Citizenship Education? What type of citizen? *Improving Schools* 4(2)

Martino W. (2001) 'Powerful people aren't usually real kind, friendly, open people!' Boys interrogating masculinities at school. In Martino W. and Meyenn B. (eds) *What about the boys?* Buckingham: Open University Press

Marton F., Dall'Alba G. and Beaty E. (1993) Conceptions of learning. *International Journal of Educational Research* 19(3)

Meier D. (1998) Authenticity and educational change. In Hargreaves A. *et al* (eds) *International Handbook of Educational Change*. Dordrecht: Kluwer

Midwinter E. (1972) *Priority education*. Harmondsworth: Penguin

Mills M. (2001) Pushing it to the max: interrogating the risky business of being a boy. In Martino W. and Meyenn B. (eds) *What about the boys?* Buckingham: Open University Press

Ministry of Education, Denmark (1995) *Samfundsfag*. (Curriculum guidelines for citizenship education)

Mitchell C. and Sackney L. (2000) *Profound improvement: building capacity for a learning community*. Lisse: Swets and Zeitlinger

Mittler P. (2000) *Working towards inclusive education*. London: David Fulton

Møller J. (2002) Democratic leadership in an age of managerial accountability. *Improving Schools* 5(1)

Morley L. and Rassool N. (1999) *School effectiveness: fracturing the discourse*. London: Falmer

Morrison K. (2002) *School leadership and complexity theory*. London: RoutledgeFalmer

Mortimore P., Sammons P., Stoll L., Lewis D. and Ecob R. (1988) *School matters: the junior years*. Wells: Open Books

Mortimore P. and Whitty G. (1997) *Can school improvement overcome the effects of disadvantages?* London: Institute of Education

National Assessment of Title 1 (1998) *Promising results, continuing challenges: final report of the National Assessment of Title 1*. Washington DC: US Department of Education

National Children's Home (2000) *NCH Factfile 2000*. London: NCH

New Community Schools. www.scotland.gov.uk/education/newcommunityschools

Nieto S. (1998) Cultural difference and educational change in a sociopolitical context. In A. Hargreaves *et al* (eds) *International handbook of educational change*. Dordrecht: Kluwer

Nieto S. (1999) *The light in their eyes: creating multicultural learning communities*. Stoke on Trent: Trentham

O'Brien T. (ed) (2001) *Enabling inclusion: Blue skies . . . dark clouds?* London: HMSO

Ofsted (1999) From failure to success. www.ofsted.gov.uk

Ofsted (2000) *Improving city schools*. London: HMSO www.ofsted.gov.uk

Ofsted (2002) Writing for inclusion. London: HMSO www.ofsted.gov.uk

OISE/UT (2001) Watching and learning 2 (www.standards.dfes.gov.uk/literacy/publications)

Ozolins U. (1979) Lawton's 'refutation' of a working-class curriculum. *Melbourne Working Papers*, 1979, University of Melbourne

Paterson L. (2002) Public-sector and independent schools in Scotland. *Improving Schools* 5(3)

Perkins D. (1992) *Smart schools: better thinking and learning for every child*. New York: The Free Press

Perkins D. (1993) Person-plus: a distributed view of thinking and learning. In Salomon G. (ed) *Distributed cognitions: psychological and educational considerations*. Cambridge: Cambridge University Press

Perkins D. (1995) *Outsmarting IQ: the emerging science of learnable intelligence*. New York: The Free Press

Petersen S. (2001) *Rituale für kooperatives Lernen in der Sekundarstufe 1*. Berlin: Cornelsen

Phi Delta Kappan www.pdkintl.org/kappan

Phillips T. (1985) Beyond lip-service – discourse development after the age of nine. In Mayor B. M. and Pugh A. K. (eds) (1987) *Language Communication and Education*. Buckingham: Open University Press

Pilling D. (1990) *Escape from disadvantage*. London: Falmer

Plummer G. (2000) *Failing working-class girls*. Stoke on Trent: Trentham

Pradl G. (ed) (1982) *Prospect and retrospect*. London: Heinemann. [writings by James Britton]

Project Zero. www.pz.harvard.edu

QCA (2001) Key Stage 3 schemes of work: Citizenship http: //www.standards.dfes.gov.uk/local/schemes/citizenship/teachguide.html

Ratzki A. (1996) *Team-Kleingruppen-modell* Köln-Holweide. Frankfurt: Lang

Rea J. and Weiner G. (1998) Cultures of blame and redemption – when empowerment becomes control. In Slee R. and Weiner G. (eds) *School effectiveness for whom?* London: Falmer

Reay D. (2002) Mothers' involvement in their children's schooling: Social Reproduction in action? *Improving Schools* 5(3)

Reay D. and Wiliam D. (1999) 'I'll be a nothing': structure, agency and the construction of identity through assessment. *British Education Research Journal* 25(3)

Rethinking schools. www.rethinkingschools.org

Reynolds D. and Teddlie C. (2001) Reflections on the critics, and beyond them. *School Effectiveness and School Improvement* 12(1)

Riddell S., Brown S. and Duffield J. (1998) The utility of qualitative research for influencing policy and practice on school effectiveness. In Slee R. and Weiner G. (eds) *School effectiveness for whom?* London: Falmer

Rieser R. (2000) Disability discrimination, the final frontier: disablement, history and liberation. In Cole M. (ed) *Education, equality and human rights.* London: Routledge

Riley K. and Macbeath J. (1998). In MacBeath J. (ed) *Effective school leadership: responding to change.* London: Chapman

Roe N. (1997) *John Keats and the culture of dissent.* Oxford: Oxford University Press

Rolff H-G. (1998) Evaluation und Schulentwicklung. In Tillman K-J. u Wischer B. (eds) *Schulinterne Evaluation an Reformschulen.* Bielefeld: Impuls

Rose H. and S. (eds) (1976) *The political economy of science: ideology in the natural sciences.* London: Macmillan

Rose S. (1998) *Lifelines: biology, freedom, determinism.* Harmondsworth: Penguin

Rose S. Kamin L. and Lewontin R. C. (1984) *Not in our genes: biology, ideology and human nature.* Harmondsworth: Penguin

Rosen H. (1972) *Language and class: a critical look at the theories of Basil Bernstein.* Bristol: Falling Wall Press

Rosenthal R. and Jacobson L. (1968) *Pygmalion in the classroom.* New York: Holt, Rinehart and Winston

Rudduck J. (1991) *Innovation and change.* Milton Keynes: Open University Press

Rudduck J. (2001) Students and school improvement. *Improving Schools* 4(2)

Russell P. (1997) Parents as partners: some early impressions of the impact of the Code of Practice. In Wolfendale S. (ed) *Working with parents after the Code of Practice.* London: David Fulton

Rutter J. (2000) *Supporting refugee children in 21st Century Britain.* Stoke on Trent: Trentham

Rutter M. *et al* (1979) *Fifteen thousand hours.* Cambridge MA: Harvard University Press

Salisbury J. and Jackson D. (1996) *Challenging macho values.* London: Falmer

Salomon G. (ed) (1993) *Distributed cognitions: psychological and educational considerations.* Cambridge: Cambridge University Press

Sammons P., Hillman J. and Mortimore P. (1995) *Key characteristics of effective schools: a review of school effectiveness research.* London: Institute of Education/Ofsted

Scheerens J. (1998) The school effectiveness knowledge base as a guide for school improvement. In Hargreaves A. *et al* (eds) *International handbook of educational change.* Dordrecht: Kluwer

Scheerens J., Bosker R. and Creemers B. (2001) Time for self-criticism: on the viability of school effectiveness research. *School Effectiveness and School Improvement* 12(1)

Schiele S. and Schneider H. (eds) (1977) *Das Konsensproblem in der politischen Bildung*. Stuttgart

Schlesinger A.J. (1991) *The disuniting of America*. New York: W. W. Norton

Scottish School Ethos Network. www.ethosnet.co.uk

Searle C. (1997) *Living community, living school: essays on education in British inner cities*. London: Tufnell Press

Searle C. (2001) *An exclusive education: race, class and exclusion in British schools*. London: Lawrence & Wishart

SEED (1998) Standard for Headship in Scotland
www.scotland.gov.uk/library5/education/sqhmp-00.asp

SEED(2002) Standard for Chartered Teachers
www.scotland.gov.uk/library5/education/sfct-00.asp

Sennett R. (1998) *The corrosion of character: the personal consequences of work in the new capitalism*. London: Norton

Sergiovanni T. (1994) *Building community in schools*. San Francisco: Jossey-Bass

Sergiovanni T. (1998) Organization, market and community as strategies for change: what works best for deep changes in schools. In Hargreaves A. *et al* (eds) *International handbook of educational change*. Dordrecht: Kluwer

Sergiovanni T. (1999) *Building community in schools*. San Francisco: Jossey-Bass

Senge P. *et al* (2000) *Schools that learn*. London: Nicholas Breasley

Sewell T. (1997) *Black masculinities and schooling: how black boys survive modern schooling*. Stoke on Trent: Trentham

Shayer M. and Adey P. (1981) *Towards a science of science teaching*. London: Heinemann

Simon B. (1955) *The common secondary school*. London: Lawrence & Wishart

Simons M. (ed) (*c*.1986) *The English curriculum: Reading 1. Comprehension*. London: English and Media Centre

Slee R. and Weiner G. with Tomlinson S. (eds) (1998) *School effectiveness for whom? Challenges to the school effectiveness and school improvement movements*. London: Falmer

Stigler J. and Hiebert J. (1999) *The teaching gap*. New York: Free Press
(also http: //www.pdkintl.org/kappan/kstg9709.htm)

Stoll L. and Fink D. (1995) *Changing our schools*. Buckingham: Open University Press

Stoll L., Fink D. and Earl L. (2003) *It's about learning (and it's about time)* London: RoutledgeFalmer

Stubbs M. (1983, 2nd edn) *Language, schools and classrooms*. London: Routledge

Sylva K. (1999) The role of research in explaining the past and shaping the future. In Abbott L. and Moylett H. (eds) *Early education transformed*. London: Falmer

Teddlie C. and Reynolds D. (2000) *International handbook of school effectiveness research*. London: RoutledgeFalmer

Teddlie C. and Reynolds D. (2001) Countering the critics: responses to recent criticisms of school effectiveness research. *School Effectiveness and School Improvement* 12(1)

Teddlie C. and Stringfield S. (1993) *Schools do make a difference: lessons learned from a 10-year study of school effects*. New York: Teachers College Press

Thomas W.P. and Collier V. (1997) *School effectiveness for language minority students*. Washington DC: National Clearinghouse for Bilingual Education

Thrupp M. (1999) *Schools making a difference: let's be realistic!: school mix, school effectiveness, and the social limits of reform*. Buckingham: Open University Press

Tomlinson S. (2002) Selection, diversity and inequality. *Improving Schools* 5(3)

Topping K. (1986) *Parents as educators: trianing parents to teach their children*. London: Croom Helm

Tyler R. (1949) *Basic principles of curriculum and instruction*. Chicago: University of Chicago Press

White J. and Barber M. (eds) (1997) *Perspectives on school effectiveness and school improvement*. London: Institute of Education

Whitty G. (1981) Curriculum studies: a critique of some recent British orthodoxies. In Lawn M. and Barton L. (eds) *Rethinking curriculum studies: a radical approach*. New York: Croom Helm

Williams R. (1961) *The long revolution*. London: Chatto & Windus

Wood E.M. (1998) Modernity, postmodernity or capitalism. In McChesney R. *et al* (eds) *Capitalism and the information age*. New York: Monthly Review Press

Woods P. and Levacic R. (2002) Raising school performance in the league tables, part 1: disentangling the effects of school disadvantage. *British Educational Research Journal* 28(2)

Wright C. (1987) 'Black students – white teacers', in Troyna B. (ed) *Racial inequality in education*. London: Routledge

Wrigley T. (1997) Raising achievement for Asian pupils. *Multicultural Teaching* 16(1)

Wrigley T. (2000) *The power to learn: stories of success in the education of Asian and other bilingual pupils*. Stoke on Trent: Trentham

Wrigley T. (2000a) Pedagogies for improving schools: an invitation to debate. *Improving Schools* 3(3)

Wrigley T. (2001) An editor visits: Spittal Primary School. *Improving Schools* 4(1)

Wrigley T. (2002) An editor visits: All Saints, Glasgow. *Improving Schools* 5(2)

Index